At Issue

Is Socialism Harmful?

Other Books in the At Issue Series:

At Issue

Is Socialism Harmful?

Ronald D. Lankford Jr., Book Editor

GREENHAVEN PRESS
A part of Gale, Cengage Learning

GALE
CENGAGE Learning

Detroit • New York • San Francisco • New Haven, Conn • Waterville, Maine • London

Christine Nasso, *Publisher*
Elizabeth Des Chenes, *Managing Editor*

For more information, contact:
Greenhaven Press
27500 Drake Rd.
Farmington Hills, MI 48331-3535
Or you can visit our Internet site at gale.cengage.com

For product information and technology assistance, contact us at

Gale Customer Support, 1-800-877-4253
For permission to use material from this text or product, submit all requests online at www.cengage.com/permissions

Further permissions questions can be emailed to permissionrequest@cengage.com

Articles in Greenhaven Press anthologies are often edited for length to meet page requirements. In addition, original titles of these works are changed to clearly present the main thesis and to explicitly indicate the author's opinion. Every effort is made to ensure that Greenhaven Press accurately reflects the original intent of the authors. Every effort has been made to trace the owners of copyrighted material.

Cover image © Images.com/Corbis.

LIBRARY OF CONGRESS CATALOGING-IN-PUBLICATION DATA

Is socialism harmful? / Ronald D. Lankford, Jr., book editor.
    p. cm. -- (At issue)
    Includes bibliographical references and index.
    ISBN 978-0-7377-5584-8 (hardcover) -- ISBN 978-0-7377-5585-5 (pbk.)
    1. Socialism--United States. I. Lankford, Ronald D., 1962- II. Title. III. Series.
    HX86.I79 2011
    335.0973--dc22

                             2011009389

Printed in the United States of America
1 2 3 4 5   15 14 13 12 11

ED160

Contents

Introduction

Although socialism has a long history in the United States, the subject rarely has been discussed in the mainstream American press. This changed, however, during the presidential election of 2008. During that time and since, a number of observers and commentators have asserted a connection between Barack Obama and socialism. Such critics have argued that President Obama had connections to socialists and communists, and that his policies as president—from health care to Wall Street bailouts—have focused on socialist practices. While Obama and his allies have denied these charges, conservative politicians such as former House Speaker Newt Gingrich continue to draw the connection.

One group that often has been left on the sidelines during these discussions, perhaps surprisingly, is the contingent of American socialists themselves. While forming only a small component of the American political system, American socialists have formed parties, issued platforms, and run candidates in both local and presidential elections for more than a hundred years. Even today, the United States has several socialist parties, including the Socialist Party USA and the Democratic Socialists of America. In 2008, while a debate was raging about one presidential candidate's connection to socialism, several of these parties ran candidates who openly endorsed socialism.

To better understand the role that socialists play within American politics, a few commentators are beginning to ask: How popular are socialist candidates in American elections? What kind of policies do American socialists advocate? And how do the practices of American socialists differ from the practices attributed to President Obama?

In the 2008 presidential election, a number of candidates ran under the banner of socialism or left-leaning platforms that advocated socialist policies. The following is a list of some of these candidates, the parties they were affiliated with, and the number of votes each earned in the election:

- Gloria La Riva (Socialism and Liberation) 6,818 votes

- Brian Moore (Liberty Union, Socialist) 6,538 votes

- Róger Calero (Socialist Workers) 5,151 votes

- James Harris (Socialist Workers) 2,424 votes

With a total of fewer than 20,000 votes, these parties and individuals offer little challenge to the Democrats or Republicans in national elections. If, however, the vote total included liberal candidates sympathetic to socialist policies—such as independent candidate Ralph Nader, who garnered 739,034 votes, and Green Party candidate Cynthia McKinney, who received 161,797 votes—the totals grow much higher.

These numbers bring the total votes to more than 900,000. And although this total remains less than 1 percent of votes cast in the 2008 election, as recently as the 2000 election Nader received nearly 3 million votes. Still, these totals amount to no more than 3 percent of the vote totals for the 2000 election. Thus, although many Americans vote for socialist and left-leaning candidates, socialists remain a small minority in the political spectrum.

In terms of policy, socialists reject the traditional role of capitalism to control markets and instead advocate that either the government or workers oversee economic policy. Likewise, socialists generally are more inclined to assign government a role in creating security in housing, health care, and the job market. The Socialist Party USA, for example, maintains the following positions on contemporary issues:

- A minimum wage of fifteen dollars per hour

- The withdrawal of American troops from Afghanistan and Iraq

- Universal health care coverage for all Americans

- The public ownership of all agricultural resources

- The dismantling of the US Department of Homeland Security

In July 2010, the Democratic Socialists of America issued a "Bill of Rights for the 21st Century." These rights included:

- Everyone has a right to earn a living wage.

- Everyone has a right to a sufficient amount of nutritious and safe food.

- Everyone has the right to affordable and safe housing.

- Everyone has the right to preventative, acute and long-term health care.

- Everyone has the right to free, high-quality public education.

How do these policies compare with those of President Obama's administration or, more broadly, the Democratic Party to which he belongs?

According to President Obama's critics, his health care legislation is clearly a case in which he is putting socialist ideas into practice. Such critics assert that legislation passed in 2009 gives government more control over health care. One section of the legislation, for example, would force many Americans to purchase health care or pay a fee for being uninsured. For critics, these policies remove free choice from American health care and create a health care system similar to the ones operated in Canada and Western Europe.

Others have suggested that President Obama's efforts to bail out Wall Street finance companies and American automakers with federal funds are based on socialist practices. With capitalism, they argue, companies either make a profit or go bankrupt. By bailing out Wall Street and American auto companies, critics contend, the government is attempting to control the economy. By refusing to allow American markets to rise and fall naturally, the government has turned its back on the freedom of capitalism and embraced the controlled markets of socialism, according to critics.

Although these policies may touch upon socialist practices, it is debatable how closely they resemble the beliefs of American socialists. For instance, most American socialists were also critical of President Obama's health care legislation, but for different reasons. American socialists argued that the new legislation did not go far enough and that under this law, privately owned insurance companies would continue to have too much power.

Likewise, American socialists argued against the government's bailing out of corporate America. For American socialists, bailing out Wall Street and the auto companies was in some respects in line with socialist policies, but because the bailouts primarily benefited the wealthy they violated basic socialist principles. Overall, when American socialists criticize the president, they criticize him for his lack of commitment to the broader principles of socialism.

The debate over socialism in America seems likely to continue. Clearly there are many ways to define socialism, just as there are many ways to define capitalism. However socialism is defined, the tradition of socialism—with political parties and candidates—remains active in the United States. Clearly, the public discussion about socialism is complex and contentious at times, and it provides an opportunity to consider a dimension of American politics that goes beyond the traditional two-party system. The viewpoints in *At Issue: Is Socialism Harmful?* present arguments in favor of and opposed to socialism and explore many facets of socialist principles.

1

Socialism Is Harmful

Bill Jenkins

Bill Jenkins is a church minister who owns a contracting business.

Building wealth requires both vision and hard work. It also frequently requires other people's money to get started, but this money comes with the catch that the borrowed money eventually be paid back with interest. Socialism does not take such concepts into account. Socialists would rather spend other people's money, failing to understand a basic economic principle—other people's money eventually runs out. The only reason socialism is popular is because it has been falsely sold. Socialists advertise that it is possible to acquire something—wealth—for nothing. The universal laws of capitalism, however, reveal that socialism never works.

As I read the headlines, I can't help but see the tendrils of socialism grasping more and more every day. And it always brings to mind my uncle, Wm. R. Duvall.

When I was a boy, my uncle was the richest man I knew. He was fond of saying, "There are three things you need to get rich: time, leverage and other people's money." I didn't know what it meant at the time, but when I got older, I wanted to hear how he made it big.

"I always knew I would be rich," he said. "Even when I didn't have two nickels to rub together."

He started out as a barber, renting a chair in another man's shop for $20 a week. "10 heads," he said, "that's all I needed. After that, every dollar was mine."

"At that point," he remarked, "all I had was time. I was making money, but I wasn't getting rich." It finally occurred to him that a real way to get ahead in barbering was to have his own shop and rent out his own chairs to other guys who were getting started in the barbering business.

So he looked high and low until he found a dumpy old place where he could afford the rent, then spent his nights and weekends fixing it up. In a couple months, he had it ready and went to work. He rented out the five chairs in the shop while he still worked at the same chair he had rented for several years. "It seemed like a risky idea to leave the spot where my customers were used to coming," he told me.

Becoming an Entrepreneur

Unfortunately, after a year, his landlord realized how good the business was and forced my uncle out. "What a setback," he said. "All these customers and nowhere to go."

His first thought was to look for a new place to rent. But then he was hit with a stroke of genius: "Own my own place, and I can't get kicked out again!" It only took him a handful of days to locate what would become his goldmine: 3 acres of land with a corner shop and two houses.

He set out his shingle in the shop, bought a trailer for $150 and moved it onto the back of the property, then rented the two little houses. He had talked the owners into selling him the whole ball of wax with 100% financing over 10 years. After he got his extra chairs rented out and moved another trailer onto the property, he was flush with cash. In the end, the property was paid off in eight years. But in the meantime he dabbled in other real estate, left the country and bought a house in Cancun where he lived as a tour guide. Years later he came back and bought a beachfront house on a local river, where he lived until just recently.

"Everybody gets the same amount of time, Billy," he would often say. "But that's not enough to get you to the top of the heap." His experience with collecting the rent from four other barbers showed him the power of leverage. His no-money-down real estate deal taught him about other people's money. And I imagine he probably watched a boatload of late-night infomercials that helped formulate his "Wealth Outline."

Socialism denies the capitalistic importance of these four pillars: wealth, time, leverage and other people's money. Instead, they corrupt them to their own destructive ends.

I have come to find that what he said (even though it was completely borrowed and not original) held a great deal of truth.

But up to this point, you're probably wondering what in the world this has to do with socialism. Seems like a pretty entrepreneurial story. Right? You are correct.

Socialism's Unclear Path

Seeing the proper working of a man and his wealth, well, that makes a counterfeit all the more easily spotted. But we could add to that story our own little adventure in currency options. The same three principles are at work. Time, leverage and other peoples' money.

But the path to wealth through socialism is not so clearly seen. As a matter of fact, it is more like a path to nowhere. Because socialism denies the capitalistic importance of these four pillars: wealth, time, leverage and other people's money. Instead, they corrupt them to their own destructive ends.

Any socialist will tell you wealth is important. As a matter of fact, that is the big carrot held out to entice people to follow such a muddleheaded plan. They will also tell you that time is important. Not because you need it to build wealth, but because you need it to spend wealth. In other words, the here-and-now is what is of the utmost importance. And you must be rich now, in order to enjoy what time you have here!

Leverage is also important to the socialist. As poor men manage their wealth very poorly (but seem to know instinctively how to manage their ballot), it is imperative to leverage out the efforts of the poor man into large voting blocks. One poor man cannot get a candidate into office. But 100,000 of them, that's a horse of a different color.

Because socialists reward those who treat money poorly and penalize those who treat money well, the system will never work.

Finally, we have the socialist's take on other people's money. They love it. They covet it. And they'll do anything to get it. Obviously it is impossible to enrich the poor men who voted for them with the candidate's own money. This is why other people's money is so critically important. Unfortunately for them, they have forgotten the words of U.K. Prime Minister Margaret Thatcher, who said, "The problem with socialism is that you eventually run out of other people's money."

Whether she actually believed that or not is a question for another day. But it still has the ring of an eternal truth.

The Universal Law of Capitalism

My uncle's understanding of other people's money was that it could be used to make money for himself. And he was right. But here is a key difference. The "other people" in my uncle's life lent him that money VOLUNTARILY, not because they were coerced. And they expected a real cash return on their funds, not just the "warm feeling" that comes from being forced to help an indolent person by way of government-run charity!

Because socialists reward those who treat money poorly and penalize those who treat money well, the system will never work. True, advocates of wealth redistribution can point to circumstances where it did "work," and where it does "work" from time to time (if only for a limited time). But I can also point to circumstances where the laws of gravity are temporarily suspended, such as when I get on a plane.

But even God will not help me if I just assume because I can fly for a few hours from here to there that I can fly forever. At some point my plane has to come back to the ground. At some point the laws of gravity will resume their authority, and I will realize that my flight and my violation of gravity's laws are coming to an end.

Capitalism is a law established by God, just like gravity. Its foundation is in the 9th Commandment, "Thou shalt not covet." I am never free to desire to take what is my neighbor's. Not his wife. Not his house. Not his lands. Not his possessions. I can trade him for them if I have something he wants more than what he has. (Except his wife, of course . . .) I can buy them from him if my offer is right. But I cannot steal (or vote) away his property into my account. That is not wealth creation; it is merely redistribution. God condemns it, and He will not be mocked by those who think that they can make socialism "fly" forever.

Eventually, they will run out of other people's money. And when they do, their plane will come crashing to the ground.

The False Advertising of Socialism

One more thing. All around us, we see the widespread push toward more socialism, even when it hasn't yet worked. How could that be? To explain what we are seeing currently, we must acknowledge that if the socialists manage to escape complete annihilation in the plane that they wreck, they will begin a campaign of propaganda, reminding the people that if only the free market force of gravity hadn't gotten involved, they would have been successful. And that all they need is more fuel (other people's money) to get the thing going again.

And, of course, the people will see the wisdom of their case, and will vote for more fuel or parts or anything, just so long as we don't let those stupid Gravitarians have control of the cockpit.

More groundbreaking efforts will be tried, such as debasing the fuel, so that we have more of it. Sure, if you add five gallons of water to five gallons of gasoline you get 10 gallons. . . . Certainly we can go further on twice as much fuel, right? Yeah, Right. Whatever you say, Comrade. Meanwhile, anybody who knows better had better be preparing a parachute.

As the major nations of the world move deeper and deeper into the "Pit of Despair" (to borrow a good term from *The Princess Bride*), their solutions will work less and less. Each effort will become more and more futile. Perhaps then we will learn our lessons. If not we will be doomed to repeat them.

2

Socialism Is Not Harmful

Democratic Socialists of America

The Democratic Socialists of America is the largest socialist organization in the United States and the principal US affiliate of the Socialist International.

Democratic socialists believe that democracy and socialism complement each other and that the corporation and the society should meet the needs of all people. The Democratic Socialists of America (DSA) do not believe that the government should own all businesses. Businesses, the DSA argues, should be operated and directed by the employees who work for them. In addition, the DSA does not believe that people will no longer be motivated to work if the profit incentive is removed—if work is meaningful, people enjoy working. Critics of socialism point out that there are no countries that fully embrace socialism, but many countries have used socialist ideas to establish such programs as universal health care and government-run literacy programs and childcare centers. Democratic socialism also offers a vision of social justice, fighting for the rights of workers, minorities, women, and the gay and lesbian communities. Although antisocialist sentiment is strong in the United States, socialists share a proud heritage in the struggle to make America a more democratic and egalitarian society.

Democratic socialists believe that both the economy and society should be run democratically—to meet public needs, not to make profits for a few. To achieve a more just

"What Is Democratic Socialism?," Democratic Socialists of America, September 20, 2010. www.dsausa.org. Copyright © 2010 by Democratic Socialists of America. All rights reserved. Reproduced by permission.

society, many structures of our government and economy must be radically transformed through greater economic and social democracy so that ordinary Americans can participate in the many decisions that affect our lives.

Democracy and socialism go hand in hand. All over the world, wherever the idea of democracy has taken root, the vision of socialism has taken root as well—everywhere but in the United States. Because of this, many false ideas about socialism have developed in the US. . . . We hope to answer some of your questions about socialism.

Doesn't socialism mean that the government will own and run everything?

Democratic socialists do not want to create an all-powerful government bureaucracy. But we do not want big corporate bureaucracies to control our society either. Rather, we believe that social and economic decisions should be made by those whom they most affect.

Today, corporate executives who answer only to themselves and a few wealthy stockholders make basic economic decisions affecting millions of people. Resources are used to make money for capitalists rather than to meet human needs. We believe that the workers and consumers who are affected by economic institutions should own and control them.

Social ownership could take many forms, such as worker-owned cooperatives or publicly owned enterprises managed by workers and consumer representatives. Democratic socialists favor as much decentralization as possible. While the large concentrations of capital in industries such as energy and steel may necessitate some form of state ownership, many consumer-goods industries might be best run as cooperatives.

Democratic socialists have long rejected the belief that the whole economy should be centrally planned. While we believe that democratic planning can shape major social investments like mass transit, housing, and energy, market mechanisms are needed to determine the demand for many consumer goods.

Hasn't socialism been discredited by the collapse of Communism in the USSR [former Soviet Union] and Eastern Europe?

Socialists have been among the harshest critics of authoritarian Communist states. Just because their bureaucratic elites called them "socialist" did not make it so; they also called their regimes "democratic." Democratic socialists always opposed the ruling party-states of those societies, just as we oppose the ruling classes of capitalist societies. We applaud the democratic revolutions that have transformed the former Communist bloc. However, the improvement of people's lives requires real democracy without ethnic rivalries and/or new forms of authoritarianism. Democratic socialists will continue to play a key role in that struggle throughout the world.

Moreover, the fall of Communism should not blind us to injustices at home. We cannot allow all radicalism to be dismissed as "Communist." That suppression of dissent and diversity undermines America's ability to live up to its promise of equality of opportunity, not to mention the freedoms of speech and assembly.

We don't agree with the capitalist assumption that starvation or greed are the only reasons people work. People enjoy their work if it is meaningful and enhances their lives.

Private corporations seem to be a permanent fixture in the US, so why work toward socialism?

In the short term we can't eliminate private corporations, but we can bring them under greater democratic control. The government could use regulations and tax incentives to encourage companies to act in the public interest and outlaw destructive activities such as exporting jobs to low-wage countries and polluting our environment. Public pressure can also have a critical role to play in the struggle to hold corporations accountable. Most of all, socialists look to unions to make private business more accountable.

Won't socialism be impractical because people will lose their incentive to work?

We don't agree with the capitalist assumption that starvation or greed are the only reasons people work. People enjoy their work if it is meaningful and enhances their lives. They work out of a sense of responsibility to their community and society. Although a long-term goal of socialism is to eliminate all but the most enjoyable kinds of labor, we recognize that unappealing jobs will long remain. These tasks would be spread among as many people as possible rather than distributed on the basis of class, race, ethnicity, or gender, as they are under capitalism. And this undesirable work should be among the best, not the least, rewarded work within the economy. For now, the burden should be placed on the employer to make work desirable by raising wages, offering benefits and improving the work environment. In short, we believe that a combination of social, economic, and moral incentives will motivate people to work.

Why are there no models of democratic socialism?

Although no country has fully instituted democratic socialism, the socialist parties and labor movements of other countries have won many victories for their people. We can learn from the comprehensive welfare state maintained by the Swedes, from Canada's national health care system, France's nationwide childcare program, and Nicaragua's literacy programs. Lastly, we can learn from efforts initiated right here in the US, such as the community health centers created by the government in the 1960s. They provided high quality family care, with community involvement in decision-making.

But hasn't the European Social Democratic experiment failed?

For over half a century, a number of nations in Western Europe and Scandinavia have enjoyed both tremendous prosperity and relative economic equality thanks to the policies pursued by social democratic parties. These nations used their relative wealth to ensure a high standard of living for their citizens—high wages, health care and subsidized education. Most importantly, social democratic parties supported strong labor movements that became central players in economic decision-making. But with the globalization of capitalism, the old social democratic model becomes ever harder to maintain. Stiff competition from low-wage labor markets in developing countries and the constant fear that industry will move to avoid taxes and strong labor regulations has diminished (but not eliminated) the ability of nations to launch ambitious economic reform on their own. Social democratic reform must now happen at the international level. Multinational corporations must be brought under democratic controls, and workers' organizing efforts must reach across borders.

Now, more than ever, socialism is an international movement. As socialists have always known, the welfare of working people in Finland or California depends largely on standards in Italy or Indonesia. As a result, we must work toward reforms that can withstand the power of multinationals and global banks, and we must fight for a world order that is not controlled by bankers and bosses.

Aren't you a party that's in competition with the Democratic Party for votes and support?

No, we are not a separate party. Like our friends and allies in the feminist, labor, civil rights, religious, and community organizing movements, many of us have been active in the Democratic Party. We work with those movements to strengthen the party's left wing, represented by the Congressional Progressive Caucus.

The process and structure of American elections seriously hurts third party efforts. Winner-take-all elections instead of proportional representation, rigorous party qualification requirements that vary from state to state, a presidential instead of a parliamentary system, and the two-party monopoly on political power have doomed third party efforts. We hope that at some point in the future, in coalition with our allies, an alternative national party will be viable. For now, we will continue to support progressives who have a real chance at winning elections, which usually means left-wing Democrats.

If I am going to devote time to politics, why shouldn't I focus on something more immediate?

Although capitalism will be with us for a long time, reforms we win now—raising the minimum wage, securing a national health plan, and demanding passage of right-to-strike legislation—can bring us closer to socialism. Many democratic socialists actively work in the single-issue organizations that advocate for those reforms. We are visible in the reproductive freedom movement, the fight for student aid, gay, lesbian, bisexual and transgendered organizations, anti-racist groups, and the labor movement.

It is precisely our socialist vision that informs and inspires our day-to-day activism for social justice. As socialists we bring a sense of the interdependence of all struggles for justice. No single-issue organization can truly challenge the capitalist system or adequately secure its particular demands. In fact, unless we are all collectively working to win a world without oppression, each fight for reforms will be disconnected, maybe even self-defeating.

Anti-socialism has been repeatedly used to attack reforms that shift power to working class people and away from corporate capital.

What can young people do to move the US toward socialism?

Since the Civil Rights movement of the 1950s, young people have played a critical role in American politics. They have been a tremendous force for both political and cultural change in this country: in limiting the US's options in the war in Vietnam, in forcing corporations to divest from the racist

South African regime, in reforming universities, and in bringing issues of sexual orientation and gender discrimination to public attention. Though none of these struggles were fought by young people alone, they all featured youth as leaders in multi-generational progressive coalitions. Young people are needed in today's struggles as well: for universal health care and stronger unions, against welfare cuts and predatory multinational corporations.

Schools, colleges and universities are important to American political culture. They are the places where ideas are formulated and policy discussed and developed. Being an active part of that discussion is a critical job for young socialists. We have to work hard to change people's misconceptions about socialism, to broaden political debate, and to overcome many students' lack of interest in engaging in political action. Off-campus, too, in our daily cultural lives, young people can be turning the tide against racism, sexism and homophobia, as well as the conservative myth of the virtue of "free" markets.

If so many people misunderstand socialism, why continue to use the word?

First, we call ourselves socialists because we are proud of what we are. Second, no matter what we call ourselves, conservatives will use it against us. Anti-socialism has been repeatedly used to attack reforms that shift power to working class people and away from corporate capital. For example National health care legislation has always been labeled as socialism by those opposed to it. Medicare was passed in spite of the name calling. In 1993 the Clinton plan was defeated in part because it was labeled "socialized medicine." In one of the great political ironies the health care legislation passed in 2010 was almost defeated by two years of socialist baiting in spite of the fact that it was largely based on proposals originally introduced by Republicans. Liberals are routinely denounced as socialists in order to discredit reform. Until we face, and beat, the stigma attached to the "S word," politics in America will continue to be stifled and our options limited. We also call ourselves socialists because we are proud of the traditions upon which we are based, of the heritage of the Socialist Party of [socialist leaders] Eugene Debs and Norman Thomas, and of other struggles for change that have made America more democratic and just. Finally, we call ourselves socialists to remind everyone that we have a vision of a better world.

3

Socialism Supports American Values

Timothy V. Gatto

Timothy V. Gatto is a retired US Army sergeant and the author of From Complicity to Contempt.

Many journalists identify political problems, but few offer solutions. Likewise, while many political writers identify themselves as liberal or socialist, few are willing to offer socialist solutions. Perhaps, however, the socialist journalist should speak out, even though many people believe that socialism is un-American. Especially in difficult economic times, however, socialism may offer solutions that could help many Americans. For instance, if the government is willing to bail out the banks that have defaulted on loans, why not bail out homeowners who have defaulted on loans? Socialism could meet the needs of everyday working people, not just the needs of Wall Street. Socialism is far from un-American, precisely because it would allow everyday people to have more control over economic issues that affect them.

The mood in America couldn't be darker. I've noticed that many articles that bemoan the current state of affairs, i.e.; the corporate control of the two major political parties and the media, the outsourcing of American jobs overseas, the waste, fraud and abuse of government and the unbridled military spending in support of major military adventures overseas that cannot be justified by logic, just to name a few, are accompanied by a persistent comment. Many readers of these articles have a comment that basically says "I know what problems we face, why aren't you suggesting solutions?"

I can understand why many political writers hesitate to put their views on what they think would offer solutions to the problems Americans face. I believe that many writers feel that it is more important for the people to understand what is happening than to offer their opinions on how to solve these issues.

I too felt this way until recently. I now believe that the majority of people that will read this article truly understand what is happening. In fact, I briefly stopped writing about what I see happening across America because I felt that I was "preaching to the choir". I found myself writing about the same things over and over again. The details may have changed, but the basic underlying causes of these problems like corporate control of the government and the mainstream media were still the same. Since 2004 I have written hundreds of articles that all expressed the same opinion. I now find myself reluctant to sit down and write another piece about it; after all, how many different ways can you tell the same old story?

Time to Offer Solutions

I believe that those that comment about articles that identify the problems but put forth no solutions may be right. I had always thought that the job of a political pundit was to make people think. I now believe that this job has been accomplished. I can remember how many readers called me a radical and insinuated that I was half-crazy just a few years ago. It's amazing how that has changed. Now I hear "OK, we know what's happening; now what are we supposed to do about it?"

There are solutions. In 2008 the United States decided to intervene to try to avert the financial sector from a giant meltdown due to their malfeasance. This didn't sit well with the people that understood that they were laying out taxpayer money to prop up a financial sector that had made a fortune preying on the people they were now asking to pull their feet from the fire. People still hold resentment over this, witness the tea-party movement and the uproar from almost everywhere.

We can see, if we care to look, exactly where our form of capitalism has gotten us.

I think that far from being such a bad thing, the intervention by the government illustrated just how capitalism works. Time and time again, when the economy contracts as it did in 2008, America has had to resort to socialist methods in order to save capitalism from imploding, but once the problems were solved, once our government put these banks on solid financial ground, they gave them back to the very people that had run them into the ground in the first place. The question I would like to ask is why?

I've noticed that many of our most popular political writers on the progressive left are socialists. Some of these writers have publically acknowledged their political affiliation and some have not. As a card-carrying socialist, I can generally tell who has socialist leanings by what they say. I can understand why some prefer not to divulge their political identity. In this nation we have a tendency to disregard socialists and socialism because of the cold war propaganda that equated socialism with communism and repressive regimes that operated under the "socialist" banner. Even though the communists never embraced true socialism as it was originally laid out, decades of anti-socialist propaganda is indelibly etched upon most American minds.

Americans Deserve a Second Chance

America has a golden opportunity to change the way we have been doing business for the last two centuries. We can see, if we care to look, exactly where our form of capitalism has gotten us. The Middle Class in America is vanishing according to our government's own numbers. We have seen the median income decrease by almost $2,000.00 per year. We have arrived at a point in our history where we practically have only two economic classes, the rich and the poor. In 1998, this country had the top 1% holding 42.9% of the nation's wealth. The next 19% had 48.4%. The bottom 80% had 8.7% of this nation's wealth. That seems horrific, does it not? That's nothing, in 2007, the top 1% had 42.7%, and the next 19% had 50.3% and 80% had only 7%. Eighty percent of the people had only 7% of the wealth! Is it any wonder that there is a strong undercurrent of resentment in this nation today?

I'm sure that we could develop an American style of socialism that would work better than the predatory capitalism we have in place now.

We are fed the same nonsense from cradle to grave with platitudes such as "You can be anything you want to be in America." "There is always room at the top for hard workers." "Everyone has the same opportunity for success."

That is pure, unadulterated crap. The other old adages certainly make more sense: "It takes money to make money"; "It's not what you know, it's who you know."

Since Uncle Sam owns something like 97% of the mortgages in this country, maybe it's time to show some "brotherly" love to our citizens. Why are so many Americans defaulting on their mortgages? Just look who is still in charge of the accounts receivable at the banks. You would think that the Federal government would demand that banks try and work better deals to stop foreclosures, after all, the same people they are foreclosing upon were the same people that bailed them out of bankruptcy! It is said that "The business of America is business." Does this mean that the banks have an unwritten rule that in order to survive they must be predators? Is it written somewhere that "If you can't pay, hit the road"? We can do better than that. It should be mandated that Americans be given a second chance to keep their homes if the financial distress they are in is through no fault of their own. After all, the banking industry got a second chance, why not the people that gave it to them?

A Socialist Solution for America

There are so many in the GOP [Republican Party] railing against the concept that government should not be of a larger "community." Where do you think that came from? They decry "generational welfare" and suggest that any government program that aids citizens in time of need is a "hand-out." Yet the financial sector just received the largest "hand-out" in U.S. history. The prevailing view in America is that "Corporations are considered to have the same rights as people." I claim that corporations have more rights than people in this country today. Thanks to the Supreme Court, corporations can effectively "buy" their very own politicians by paying all of their election bills. Our elected officials will now have outright corporate sponsorship with no restrictions. Just who will they be representing, the people or their benefactor corporations?

Socialism works from the bottom up. The banks we bailed out should be run by the citizens that bailed them out, not the people that helped create the mess we had to bail them out of. Oversight committees that represent the interests of our citizens should have been in place by now. The same story for GM [General Motors] and Chrysler; since the government bailed them out, they should have sold the companies to the workers. Instead, unions have to force pay cuts upon their members and take responsibility for funding their major medical insurance. GM says it paid the government back with interest. Before you start believing in miracles, let me tell you that they just paid America back with another loan.

I'm not arguing that the United States should adopt socialism overnight, but I'm sure that we could develop an American style of socialism that would work better than the predatory capitalism we have in place now. I can see a system where small businesses and individuals remain under the capital system, but that banks and other financial entities and companies "too big to fail" should be under citizen controlled socialism. I'm sure the Republicans and conservatives and all of the people that believe in "American exceptionalism" will have a field day with this article. Still, readers asked for solutions and I put forth mine. If you can't count on the people to run things the right way, just stick with the wonderful "corporate model" that has been rammed down our throats since our inception. Take the power out of the hands of the corporations and give it back to the people. Is that un-American? I don't think so.

Socialism Does Not Support American Values

Rick Pedraza

Rick Pedraza is a writer for NewsMax, an online media organization.

In recent years, a number of Americans have expressed a growing fear that socialism is gaining ground in the United States. Senator Jim DeMint of South Carolina expresses this view in his book Saving Freedom. *As the federal government has grown, its powers have overreached the original intent of the Constitution. The growth of government became more pronounced with the birth of the welfare state under President Franklin Delano Roosevelt during the 1930s and 1940s. As Americans have become comfortable with government control, they have forgotten that the United States was founded on principles of freedom. To return to these principles, Americans must take personal responsibility, volunteering in communities and persuading their state governments to assume control over public education, health care, and energy.*

Sen. Jim DeMint, R-S.C. [Republican, South Carolina], is sounding an alarm for all Americans amidst worries that the "land of the free" and "home of the brave" is turning to socialism. In his new book, *Saving Freedom*, he urges Americans to reclaim their freedom and outlines a plan to return America to its founding principles.

"It's become more and more apparent to me that too many Americans don't understand why we have been exceptional as a country, why we've been prosperous, and why we've been good as a nation," DeMint tells Newsmax.TV.

A Limited Federal Government

DeMint, whose new book has been compared to a new Declaration of Independence, says he decided to write it because the concept of freedom has been a part of America since the very beginning.

The basic idea of constitutional government has been abandoned.

"Now the lines between what we do as a free society and what the government should do have been so blurred that people seem willing to accept government intervention into almost every area of our lives," he says.

DeMint wants Americans to once again understand what freedom is, how it works, and how government has never been further from it.

"The basic idea of constitutional government has been abandoned," he says. "The Constitution limits what the federal government can do, but we ignore that every day and start new programs that have nothing to do with those powers that were given to the federal government in the Constitution."

DeMint says America is moving away from the rule of law and that some of the laws passed recently are, in effect, retroactive. He notes government is going back and changing laws that were in place for years.

"We are drifting as the government takes over more and more areas of our economy. We know they run education; they're trying to take over health care; they're in the banking and finance business now, they control our energy; and they want to take over more and more almost every day."

America's Move Toward Socialism

DeMint's new book describes a socialist movement under way in the United States that is happening so slowly that most Americans don't recognize it. He says the signs toward socialism have been going on since the ink on the Constitution dried, but it really started in full force with FDR [President Franklin Delano Roosevelt] and the New Deal after World War II [*sic*].

"Americans were looking for some security from government, and that's when we began to expand the entitlement programs of Social Security and later got to Medicare," he explains.

"We expanded protections of unions and a lot of things that are collectivist. But we've seen since the Great Depression an expanding role of the federal government that continues to this day."

DeMint likens the erosion of freedom and, subsequently, the economic and political strength that came with it, to the story he tells in the book about the gingerbread man who trusts the fox to take him across the river. At first the gingerbread man sits on the fox's back, but when the fox begins to sink, he moves to the neck, then the tip of the nose, and then the fox eats him.

We just need to recognize what makes America work—and that is freedom. It's not government.

"It's a pretty good analogy as far as what we're doing as a people," DeMint says about allowing the government to do more and more to the point where the American people are too dependent to do things themselves.

"This is the eleventh hour," he warns. "And I'm afraid if Americans don't stand up now, this congress and this president are going to move us to the left of Europe to more of a socialized economy and culture."

DeMint says the dangers that [lurk] with a move toward socialism include chronically high unemployment and an economy that does not grow at nearly the pace it has in the past. He notes how the big government approach that took hold in Europe and other countries has paralyzed the growth of their economies.

"We're going to move more towards these other countries if we're not careful," DeMint tells Newsmax. "We just need to recognize what makes America work—and that is freedom. It's not government. Government did not make our country great and I'm afraid it's going to sink us if we don't stop government's growth right now!"

Taking Personal Responsibility

DeMint notes that today a lot of young Americans are raised in government schools and liberal universities, and unless they've actually had the chance to participate in a free market economy as he did for years, more people will see government as the center of the American culture and economics.

"That's not the way it works," he says. "I'm afraid a lot of people just don't understand where we are."

In the closing chapter of *Saving Freedom*, DeMint outlines an action plan that starts with the individual. It encourages every individual to take responsibility for themselves.

"As we look at the health care of our nation, we've got to look at our own health care and the health care of family— what we can do to lower the cost of health care just by taking care of ourselves; what we can do by volunteering in the community and doing things that help people who are poor so government doesn't have to do it; what we can insist our state governments do to take back control of education and health care and energy; and then what we can expect our federal politicians to do."

DeMint recommends more education choice. He is convinced that if America allows its children to continue to be educated in government schools, it will cease to be a free nation.

"I propose and promote the idea of this road map to the future that Congressman Paul Ryan [R-Wisc.] has put together which reforms our tax code, social security and our health care system. It keeps the promise of Medicare and social security, but it gives people a lot more choices—and the government spends less money to do it."

5

Barack Obama Is a Socialist

Larry Thornberry

Larry Thornberry is a Florida-based writer who has written for the American Spectator.

With the Democrats in control of the White House, Senate, and House of Representatives at the beginning of Barack Obama's second year as president, political opponents frequently label Democratic policies as socialist. While the word often is used rhetorically as an insult, a closer look at the policies of President Obama and other Democrats reveals a deeper truth: Although the Democrats may not be socialists technically, it is difficult to separate their guiding principles from socialism's. Socialists wish to control all aspects of life, from popular culture to economics. Since Obama and his political allies enact legislation that seeks greater control of how Americans live, there is little to distinguish these practices from the practices of a socialist government.

In toney, left-wing circles it's considered rude, as well as prima-facie evidence of yahooism or worse, to suggest that [President Barack] Obama, [House Speaker Nancy] Pelosi, [Senate Majority Leader Harry] Reid, and the rest of the merry majority in Washington today are socialists. Conversations with liberals either end or get testy when this word comes up. The charge of socialism, they huff, is too outrageous to even consider.

A primo example of this came on one of the yak-yak shows Sunday morning [January 17, 2010,] where uber-liberal [journalist] Bob Woodward of the "Washington Pest" pronounced that calling Obama a socialist is "not even in the ballpark" (Bob apparently being unaware that Obama's ball park only has a left field).

Closer to home I have a dear friend who's a trial lawyer in Tampa [Florida] where I live and who voted for our rookie president (in accordance with a strict work rule of the trial lawyers' union). He tells me he quits reading commentary on the current scene when he encounters the word socialism. My guess is he would put his fingers in his ears if I brought the word up in conversation, though he is, taken all around, a most gracious fellow.

Some of the more acute on the left realize the socialist label is apt enough and only ham it up in this wise because they know most Americans—saving a large fraction of those in academe, most of the media, Hollywood, the mainline clergy, most foundations, the education industry, environmentalists, and the literati—don't fancy socialism, or politicians who promote it.

Is It Fair to Call Democrats Socialists?

Of course most of this lefty behavior is based on attitude rather than analysis. It's more a matter of etiquette than polemics [an argument made against a person or doctrine]. The folks tuning out references to socialism are treating the word as a mere insult and don't bother to parse whether this is or isn't an accurate designation for what the current post-everything administration is all about.

So, is it? In trying to sort out this thorny problem of political definition I look for guidance to—as I often do in dealing with life's more perplexing questions—one of [actor] John Wayne's movies. The Duke doesn't let me down.

In 1959's *Rio Bravo*, the Duke is the sheriff and [actor] Dean Martin plays his deputy, a guy who's quick and slick with a gun when he's sober. In one scene, Martin's character asks the sheriff if he thought he, the Martin character, was as good and as fast as another gunman. The Duke takes a thoughtful beat, as he was so good at doing, and replies, "Well, I'd hate to have to make a living on the difference."

Well now there you are. Thanks again, Duke. What Obama and his legions are doing may not exactly be socialism, which is usually defined as government ownership of the means of production. But when you try to contrast socialism with what Obama and his crowd have put through and what they're whooping up, if you seek to isolate real differences between socialism and Obamaism, it would be awfully hard, as the Duke phrased it, to make a living on the difference.

Socialist Policies

Consider. The Obama administration and its congressional courtiers have put the federal government into the domestic car business in a big way. They've gotten "health care" legislation through both federal houses that goes a long way toward nationalizing one-sixth of the economy, they put the national debt on steroids, and they're going for the homerun in cap and trade legislation, which would take decisions on how much and what kind of energy can be used in the economy from the private sector where they belong and turn them over to politicians and bureaucrats.

Government making all the decisions—economic, political, cultural, sexual, religious, personal—is what socialism is all about.

Cap and trade, if enacted, would effectively Sovietize the United States. America under cap and trade would have a command and control economy run (into the ground) out of Washington. As for America's long run of affluence and liberty, it would be time for Dandy Don [Meredith, former *Monday Night Football* color commentator who when he thought the game had been clinched by one of the contending teams would] sing, "Turn out the light, the party's over." Cap and trade America would be grotesquely different than what America is and ever has been.

Likely what's happened is that modern socialists have gotten smarter, or at least cagier. Contemporary socialists, in contrast to those boring old Mustache Pete socialists of decades ago who wanted to run factories and mines and mills and stuff, have figured out that actually owning the means of production is a lot of trouble, and takes away valuable time that could be more (excuse the expression) profitably spent dominating the culture. Far easier to allow some poor sod to have his name on a title somewhere and think he owns the factory (or restaurant, or car dealership, or contracting business, or, or, or . . .) and just make all the important decisions for him. Call this soft-socialism, smart-socialism, or perhaps just lazy-socialism.

Plus there's the matter that people who own businesses often face losses. Better to take the profits in taxes and let the "owner" absorb the losses.

Socialism and Government Control

As we've seen, this goes well beyond economics. Government making all the decisions—economic, political, cultural, sexual, religious, personal—is what socialism is all about. Under socialism *everything* is political.

The depressing tendency toward over-regulation, a fact of life at least since the New Deal, has gone into warp-speed with the new Washington crowd. This bunch recognizes no limits in telling business "owners" what they can produce, how much of it and when, with what kind of and how much energy, who they must hire, what they must pay employees and what conditions of employment they must provide.

As we watch Obama and his merry band annex more and more of our personal and economic freedoms by putting more and more under the federal thumb, how much comfort can be taken by saying, "Well, at least it's not exactly socialism?" Socialism vs. Obamaism may not be a distinction without a difference. But it's certainly a distinction with such a trifling difference that there's not nearly enough there to make a living on.

Could any of this be why Obama's approval rating is now well below 50 percent and his disapproval rating is higher than any Gallup has ever measured at the beginning of a president's second year? Could it also be why Republican Scott Brown is looking like a possible winner tomorrow in Massachusetts (where you could get all the state's Republicans on a single school bus and have room left over to seat the New England Patriots, in uniform)?

[Editor's note: Brown did win the election to the late Ted Kennedy's US Senate seat.]

6

Barack Obama Is Not a Socialist

Billy Wharton

Billy Wharton is the editor of the Socialist, *the national publication for the Socialist Party USA.*

Before and after the election of Barack Obama, a number of conservative politicians and news programs made the assertion that the president was a socialist. At least one political group, however, denied this assertion: American socialists. Despite conservatives' calling President Obama a socialist, none of his policies follows socialist ideas. Whether one considers banking, health care, or military commitments, all of the president's policies deviate from socialist practices. Socialists, however, believe that Obama should consider socialist policies. Only then can the government begin to address fundamental inequalities in American society.

It took a massive global financial crisis, a failed military adventure and a popular repudiation of the Republican Party to make my national television debut possible. After 15 years of socialist political organizing—everything from licking envelopes and handing out leaflets to the more romantic task of speaking at street demonstrations—I found myself in the midtown Manhattan studio of the Fox Business Network on a cold February evening. Who ever thought that being the editor of the *Socialist* magazine, circulation 3,000, would launch me on a cable news career?

The media whirlwind began in October [2008] with a call from a *New York Times* writer. He wanted a tour of the Socialist Party USA's national office. Although he was more interested in how much paper we used in our "socialist cubby hole" than in our politics, our media profile exploded. Next up, a pleasant interview by Swedish National Radio. Then Brian Moore, our 2008 presidential candidate, sparred with Stephen Colbert [comic anchor of TV's *The Colbert Report*]. Even the *Wall Street Journal* wanted a socialist to quote after the first bailout bill failed last fall. Traffic to our Web site multiplied, e-mail inquiries increased and meetings with potential recruits to the Socialist Party yielded more new members than ever before. Socialism—an idea with a long history—suddenly seemed to have a bright future in 21st-century America.

A Media Frenzy

Whom did we have to thank for this moment in the spotlight? Oddly enough, Republican politicians such as Mike Huckabee and John McCain had become our most effective promoters. During his campaign, the ever-desperate McCain, his hard-charging running mate Sarah Palin and even a plumber named Joe lined up to call Barack Obama a "socialist." Last month [February 2009], Huckabee even exclaimed that, "The Union of Soviet Socialist Republics may be dead, but the Union of American Socialist Republics is being born."

The funny thing is, of course, that socialists know that Barack Obama is not one of us.

We appreciated the newfound attention. But we also cringed as the debate took on the hysterical tone of a farcical McCarthyism.[1] The question "Is Obama a socialist?" spread

---

1. McCarthyism, named for Republican senator Joseph McCarthy, refers to a period of intense anti-Communist sentiment during the late 1940s and 1950s, a time when unfounded accusations of disloyalty destroyed many reputations.

rapidly through a network of rightwing blogs, conservative television outlets and alarmist radio talk shows and quickly moved into the mainstream. "We Are All Socialists Now," declared a *Newsweek* cover last month. A *New York Times* reporter recently pinned Obama down with the question, "Are you a socialist, as some people have suggested?" The normally unflappable politician stumbled through a response so unconvincing that it required a follow-up call in which Obama claimed impeccable free market credentials.

All this speculation over whether our current president is a socialist led me into the sea of business suits, BlackBerrys and self-promoters in the studio at Fox Business News. I quickly realized that the antagonistic anchor David Asman had little interest in exploring socialist ideas on bank nationalization. For Asman, nationalization was merely a code word for socialism. Using logic borrowed from the 1964 thriller *The Manchurian Candidate*, he portrayed Obama as a secret socialist, so far undercover that not even he understood that his policies were de facto socialist. I was merely a cudgel to be wielded against the president—a physical embodiment of guilt by association.

Obama's Lack of Socialist Credentials

The funny thing is, of course, that socialists know that Barack Obama is not one of us. Not only is he not a socialist, he may in fact not even be a liberal. Socialists understand him more as a hedge-fund Democrat—one of a generation of neoliberal politicians firmly committed to free-market policies.

The first clear indication that Obama is not, in fact, a socialist, is the way his administration is avoiding structural changes to the financial system. Nationalization is simply not in the playbook of Treasury Secretary Timothy Geithner and his team. They favor costly, temporary measures that can easily be dismantled should the economy stabilize. Socialists support nationalization and see it as a means of creating a banking system that acts like a highly regulated public utility. The banks would then cease to be sinkholes for public funds or financial versions of casinos and would become essential to re-energizing productive sectors of the economy.

The same holds true for health care. A national health insurance system as embodied in the single-payer health plan reintroduced in legislation this year by Rep. John Conyers Jr. (D-Mich.) makes perfect sense to us. That bill would provide comprehensive coverage, offer a full range of choice of doctors and services and eliminate the primary cause of personal bankruptcy—health-care bills. Obama's plan would do the opposite. By mandating that every person be insured, Obama-Care would give private health insurance companies license to systematically underinsure policyholders while cashing in on the moral currency of universal coverage. If Obama is a socialist, then on health care, he's doing a fairly good job of concealing it.

If Obama is a socialist, then ... he's doing a fairly good job of concealing it.

Issues of war and peace further weaken the commander in chief's socialist credentials. Obama announced that all U.S. combat brigades will be removed from Iraq by August 2010, but he still intends to leave as many as 50,000 troops in Iraq and wishes to expand the war in Afghanistan and Pakistan. A socialist foreign policy would call for the immediate removal of all troops. It would seek to follow the proposal made recently by an Afghan parliamentarian, which called for the United States to send 30,000 scholars or engineers instead of more fighting forces.

Obama Is Not a Socialist

Yet the president remains "the world's best salesman of socialism," according to Republican Sen. Jim DeMint of South Carolina. DeMint encouraged supporters "to take to the streets to stop America's slide into socialism." Despite the fact that billions of dollars of public wealth are being transferred to private corporations, Huckabee still felt confident in proposing that "Lenin and Stalin would love" Obama's bank bailout plan.

Huckabee is clearly no socialist scholar, and I doubt that any of Obama's policies will someday appear in the annals of socialist history. The president has, however, been assigned the unenviable task of salvaging a capitalist system intent on devouring itself. The question is whether he can do so without addressing the deep inequalities that have become fundamental features of American society. So, President Obama, what I want to know is this: Can you lend legitimacy to a society in which 5 percent of the population controls 85 percent of the wealth? Can you sell a health-care reform package that will only end up enriching a private health insurance industry? Will you continue to favor military spending over infrastructure development and social services?

My guess is that the president will avoid these questions, further confirming that he is not a socialist except, perhaps, in the imaginations of an odd assortment of conservatives. Yet as the unemployment lines grow longer, the food pantries emptier and health care scarcer, socialism may be poised for a comeback in America. The doors of our "socialist cubby-hole" are open to anyone, including Obama. I encourage him to stop by for one of our monthly membership meetings. Be sure to arrive early to get a seat—we're more popular than ever lately.

7

Socialized Medicine Offers Many Advantages

Matt Welch

Matt Welch is Reason *magazine's editor in chief.*

Although many people may object to government's involvement in health care, socialized health care like the system in France does have advantages. Compared with American health care, health care in France is less expensive and more accessible. While a person can be denied health care coverage in the United States for minor reasons, everyone is covered in France. In a modern economy where people change jobs frequently, many Americans can find themselves temporarily without insurance. This would never happen in France. Although President Barack Obama's plans may not resolve the problems of American health care, opponents must at least acknowledge that there are serious shortcomings in the current system.

By now I'm accustomed to being the only person in any given room with my particular set of cockamamie politics. But even within the more familiar confines of the libertarian movement, I am an awkward outlier on the topic of the day—health care.

To put it plainly, when free marketers warn that Democratic health care initiatives will make us more "like France," a big part of me says, "I wish." It's not that I think it's either feasible or advisable for the United States to adopt a single-payer, government-dominated system. But it's instructive to confront the comparative advantages of one socialist system abroad to sharpen the arguments for more capitalism at home.

For a dozen years now I've led a dual life, spending more than 90 percent of my time and money in the U.S. while receiving 90 percent of my health care in my wife's native France. On a personal level the comparison is no contest: I'll take the French experience any day. ObamaCare opponents often warn that a new system will lead to long waiting times, mountains of paperwork, and less choice among doctors. Yet on all three of those counts the French system is significantly *better*, not worse, than what the U.S. has now.

French vs. US Health Care

Need a prescription for muscle relaxers, an anti-fungal cream, or a steroid inhaler for temporary lung trouble? In the U.S. you have to fight to get on the appointment schedule of a doctor within your health insurance network (I'll conservatively put the average wait time at five days), then have him or her scrawl something unintelligible on a slip of paper, which you take to a drugstore to exchange for your medicine. You might pay the doc $40, but then his office sends you a separate bill for the visit, and for an examination, and those bills also go to your insurance company, which sends you an adjustment sheet weeks after the doctor's office has sent its third payment notice. By the time it's all sorted out, you've probably paid a few hundred dollars to three different entities, without having a clue about how or why any of the prices were set.

In France, by contrast, you walk to the corner pharmacist, get either a prescription or over-the-counter medication right away, shell out a dozen or so euros, and you're done. If you need a doctor, it's not hard to get an appointment within a day or three, you make payments for everything (including X-rays) on the spot, and the amounts are routinely less than the co-payments for U.S. doctor visits. I've had back X-rays, detailed ear examinations, even minor oral surgery, and never have I paid more than maybe €300 for any one procedure.

In France, you are covered, period.

And it's not like the medical professionals in France are chopped liver. In the U.S., my wife had some lumps in her breast dismissed as harmless by a hurried, indifferent doctor at Kaiser Permanente. Eight months later, during our annual Christmas visit in Lyon, one of the best breast surgeons in the country detected that the lumps were growing and removed them.

We know that the horrific amount of third-party gobble-dygook in America, the cost insensitivity, and the price randomness are all products of bad policies that market reforms could significantly improve. We know, too, that France's low retail costs are subsidized by punitively high tax rates that will have to increase unless benefits are cut. If you are rich and sick (or a healthy doctor), you're likely better off here [in the United States]. But as long as the U.S. remains this ungainly public-private hybrid, with ever-tighter mandates producing ever-fewer consumer choices, the average consumer's health care experience will probably be more pleasing in France.

Health Care for Everyone

What's more, none of these anecdotes scratches the surface of France's chief advantage, and the main reason socialized medicine remains a perennial temptation in this country: In France, you are covered, period. It doesn't depend on your job, it doesn't depend on a health maintenance organization, and it doesn't depend on whether you filled out the paperwork right. Those who (like me) oppose ObamaCare, need to understand (also like me, unfortunately) what it's like to be serially rejected by insurance companies even though you're perfectly healthy. It's an enraging, anxiety-inducing, indelible experience, one that both softens the intellectual ground for increased government intervention and produces active resentment toward anyone who argues that the U.S. has "the best health care in the world."

Since 1986 I've missed exactly three days of work due to illness. I don't smoke, I don't (usually) do drugs or drink to excess, and I eat a pretty healthy diet. I have some back pain now and then from a protruding disc, but nothing too serious. And from 1998 to 2001, when I was a freelancer in the world's capital of freelancers (Los Angeles), I couldn't get health insurance.

Kaiser rejected me because I had visited the doctor too many times in the 12 months preceding my application (I filled in the "3–5 times" circle, to reflect the three routine and inexpensive check-ups I'd had in France). Blue Cross rejected me too. There weren't many other options. Months later, an insurance broker told me I'd ruined my chances by failing to file a written appeal. "You're basically done in California," he said. "A rejection is like an arrest—if you don't contest it, you're guilty, and it's on your permanent record."

It wasn't as if I wanted or needed to consume much health care then. I was in my early 30s, and I wanted to make sure a catastrophic illness or injury wouldn't bankrupt my family. When I finally found a freelance-journalist collective that allowed me and my wife to pay $212 a month to hedge against a car accident, it a) refused to cover pregnancies or childbirths at any price and b) hiked the monthly rate up to $357 after a year. One of the main attractions of moving from freelance status to a full-time job was the ability to affix a stable price on my health insurance.

The Shortcomings of American Health Care

This is the exact opposite of the direction in which we should be traveling in a global just-in-time economy, with its ideal of entrepreneurial workers breaking free of corporate command and zipping creatively from project to project. Don't even get me started on the Kafkaesque ordeal of switching jobs without taking any time off, yet going uncovered by anything except COBRA [congressional act that allows workers to maintain health insurance during gaps in employment] for nearly two months even though both employers used the same health insurance provider. That incident alone cost me thousands of dollars I wouldn't have paid if I had controlled my own insurance policy.

I've now reached the age where I will better appreciate the premium skill level of American doctors and their high-quality equipment and techniques. And in a very real way my family has voted with its feet when it comes to choosing between the two countries. One of France's worst problems is the rigidity and expense that comes with an extensive welfare state.

But as you look at [various] health care solutions . . . , ask yourself an honest question: Are we better off today, in terms of health policy, than we would have been had we acknowledged more loudly 15 years ago that the status quo is quite awful for a large number of Americans? Would we have been better off focusing less on waiting times in Britain, and more on waiting times in the USA? It's a question I plan to ask my doctor this Christmas. In French.

8

US Health Care Reform Is Not Socialism

Amanda Marcotte

Amanda Marcotte is the author of It's a Jungle Out There *and writes about politics at Pandagon.net.*

When President Barack Obama and Democrats tried to pass health care reform legislation, many Republicans insisted on labeling this reform as socialist. Unfortunately, these opponents of health care reform purposely misused the word socialism, *leaving some listeners with the impression that health care reform would lead to a Communist dictatorship in the United States. In truth, most contemporary economies in Europe as well as that of the United States rely on a combination of free enterprise and public ownership. In the United States, for example, the public school system is funded and operated by the government. Few people, however, refer to public school as socialist. While health care reform would involve government intervention, private enterprise would continue to be an important component of health care in the United States. Referring to health care reform as socialism, then, is both misleading and disingenuous.*

As the debate over health care reform heats up this summer [2009], I'm in grave danger of tearing my hair directly out of my head if I hear the word "socialism" one more time. Look, every time the word "socialism" crops up, your internal lie detector should sound a code red.

People who use the word "socialism" to describe anything that the Democrats are proposing with regards to health care either don't know what the word "socialism" means, or are cynically exploiting the former group's ignorance. Republican National Committee [RNC] chairman Michael Steele has made his contempt for the average intelligence of his own voting base clear. When an audience member asked Steele during a recent speech if Obama's health care plan was socialism, Steele simply answered, "Yes. Next question."

It's hard to decide what's more insulting—that Steele thinks it's appropriate to lie so blatantly, or that he thinks that the public is too stupid to notice that he's lying. Unfortunately, a whole lot of people out there really do think that we're one health-care-reform bill away from living under a communist dictatorship.

Most people screaming "socialism" don't have a problem with free highways or public schools, making them socialists in their own right.

Charges of "socialism" are popular with conservatives trying to find easy, if mindless, ways to denounce universal health care. In part, it's because it's hard to know how to respond. Do you start asking people what they think socialism is and try to assess what they think the dangers of it are, or do you just deny that any of the potential bills have any relationship to this so-called socialism? Both strategies have their pluses and minuses....

Some tactics for dealing with the question of socialism:

1) *Define* socialism *and then discover what's so wrong with it.* Most people fling the word *socialism* around to describe a system much like that in Western Europe—nations that have a strong social safety net and a lot of labor protection. *Socialism* is used to describe England's National Health Services, France's 35-hour work week (with five weeks paid vacation), or the

tuition-free universities in countries like Germany. But the existence of these benefits doesn't make Europe any more socialist than the United States.

Why not? Well, just like the U.S., most European countries have an economic mix where some parts of the economy are run by the state and some are left to private enterprise, and some are a bit of both. The U.S., in fact, has "socialized" education through high school, "socialized" highway systems, and even "socialized" fire departments. Most people screaming "socialism" don't have a problem with free highways or public schools, making them socialists in their own right. And yet, capitalism hasn't gone away. Spending two or three minutes in Paris or London, where advertising is as prevalent as it is in New York City or L.A., would confirm this to any reasonable person.

2) *Point out that there's nothing "socialist" about the proposed health-care reform.* The cry of "socialism" is there to hoodwink you into thinking that the Democrats are trying to move us to a single-payer system, such as the one they have in Great Britain, where the government provides your health care for free, and everyone's on the same plan. This would be great from my point of view, but sadly, it's not what they're actually proposing.

Instead, it's a hodge-podge of reforms designed to make sure more people can buy private insurance, mainly by limiting what an insurance company can dump you for. There's also a good chance we'll be allowed to buy a publicly owned insurance similar to Medicaid, which should warm the hearts of anyone who believes that we should have more choice. Republicans trying to shut down this option are simply removing a choice from your plate and forcing you to go with private if you don't want it. But it's completely silly to pretend that a plan centered around making sure you can keep your private insurance is "socialist."

A quick perusal of the RNC's Web site opposing universal health care shows that they fully intend to fight back through disinformation and outright lies. That includes the banner picture showing a line out the door of the emergency room. Obviously, the intent is to make you think that if everyone is insured, they'll all go to emergency rooms and clog up the waiting room—instead of what? Does the RNC actually think that people without insurance will stay at home and die instead of going to the E.R.?

In truth, universal health care would do a lot to cut down on waiting times in the E.R. And a lot of people who typically use the E.R. as primary health care would be able to go to a regular doctor before their situations became dire if they had insurance. If waiting times for hospital treatment are your concern, then you should be a supporter of universal health care. And if the opponents of health care are being deceitful about that, what else are they being less than truthful about?

9

The Wall Street Bailouts Were Socialism for the Wealthy

Joseph A. Palermo

Joseph A. Palermo is an associate professor of American history at California State University, Sacramento.

Since the beginning of the 1980s, conservatives have championed one idea: getting government off the backs of the people. Less government also meant less regulation for businesses. Instead of prosperity, however, less regulation led to massive fraud. Ironically, the same proponents of smaller government—the tycoons of Wall Street—have been more than willing to accept government intervention in the form of bailouts from Washington during the recent financial crisis. While it might be tempting to allow these businesses to fail or go bankrupt for their misdeeds, this would only create further economic hardship for Americans. The only solution is for the government to reestablish its responsibility to regulate the financial sector, creating a safety net that protects Americans from the excesses of greedy business practices.

For twenty-eight years, since the beginning of [President] Ronald Reagan's first term [in 1981], we have been subjected to a steady stream of Republican propaganda claiming that if we just get government out of the way and "off our backs," deregulate the economy, and let the market work its magic, prosperity would "trickle down" to the average American citizen. In the mid-1980s, corporate lobbyists descended on Washington, threw huge amounts of campaign cash around, and told us that deregulating the Savings and Loan industry would be a great idea. [Senators] John McCain and his good friend Charles Keating from Arizona were big advocates of this scheme that turned out to be a disaster that cost taxpayers $160 billion. Phil Gramm, when he was Senator from Texas (and John McCain's choice for president in 1996), worked up another "deregulation" bill that President Bill Clinton signed into law in 1999 that repealed the Glass-Steagall Act of 1933, thereby destroying a key firewall between commercial and investment banks.

We witness the same over-confident, smug market fundamentalists and laissez-faire devotees, businessmen and -women who hate "government" when it provides aid to families with dependent children, or food stamps, or health coverage for poor people—businessmen and -women denounce as creeping "Socialism" any attempt by the government to redistribute some of the nation's wealth to the working middle class or to the poor—now come to Washington, hat in hand, begging the federal government to fix their self-created problems brought on by their own unbridled greed and recklessness and demanding massive infusions of tax-payer dollars in the form of bail out after bail out.

The laissez-faire proponents for the past thirty years have perpetrated the biggest lie ever told to the American people.

It's Socialism for the rich and laissez-faire capitalism for everybody else.

A Catastrophe in the Making

What [financial institutions] Bear Stearns, Lehman Brothers, Merrill Lynch, and now American International Group Corporation have in common is that they all hired Washington lobbyists and lavished campaign donations on politicians to push through with no public support the radical deregulation of the financial sector. Then they proceeded to create entire new categories of "financial products," derivatives and the like, that amounted to nothing but a giant Ponzi scheme [fraudulent investment scheme]. And when it all collapsed due to their Wild West, shoot 'em up, freebooting, 19th Century–style rapacious business practices, they turn to the government for a hand out to keep the whole . . . system from descending into another Great Depression.

For historians like myself, and for people like [commentators] Kevin Phillips, William Greider, and other observers, this collapse of our financial sector was like watching a slow motion train wreck. The laissez-faire proponents for the past thirty years have perpetrated the biggest lie ever told to the American people. And [President] George W. Bush, as with everything else, took this lie to its extreme. He gave the financial industry everything it wanted, and he appointed their lackeys and puppets to run the regulatory agencies that were set up in the wake of the Great Depression to avert exactly the kind of catastrophe that we're witnessing on Wall Street today [in 2008].

Ronald Reagan is often looked upon as the Republicans' Franklin Roosevelt. But Reagan sold the nation a bag of goods.

George W. Bush spent the first months of his second term on a 60-city tour where he answered prefabricated questions in phony "town hall" meetings claiming that privatizing Social Security—taking $1 trillion out of the trust fund and throwing it to his backers on Wall Street—would be a great idea. And even though the Republicans ran the House of Representatives with [Speaker] Denny Hastert and [majority leader] Tom DeLay, and the Senate with [majority leader] Bill Frist, and the presidency, the American people did not fall for this legalized form of grand larceny. And it's a good thing they didn't. Had Bush been able to get his way and throw a third of the Social Security trust fund at these same damaged, greedy firms we would be witnessing with the current financial meltdown the demise of Social Security.

The Need for More Regulation

The libertarians like Ron Paul, Bob Barr and others tell us that the government should not bail out these Wall Street hucksters and gangsters and should let them go down and pay the price for their own mismanagement and bad investments. I agree philosophically with this point of view. But I don't think it's realistic unless one is willing to see the nation enter an economic collapse that would probably look a lot like what Japan and Argentina endured in the late 1990s only worse. The fact is these giant firms, with their billionaire owners and their army of pin-striped men driving Jaguars and flying in private jets to their summer homes to visit their mistresses, have a stranglehold on the nation. They are too big to fail because it would bring on another Great Depression.

Everybody knows that what is needed is exactly, the opposite from what we've had for the past three decades. Instead of a government that is asleep at the switch and filled with cronies and hacks from the industries that are supposed to be subject to oversight, we need an activist state that rebuilds the firewalls between the commercial and investment banks; we need a "re-regulation" of the economy, especially key sectors that the entire nation depends on—finance, energy, health care, food etc. In short, what we need is a "New" New Deal in this country. We need an IRS [Internal Revenue Service] and a Justice Department that can strike fear in the hearts of these captains of industry.

Ronald Reagan is often looked upon as the Republicans' Franklin Roosevelt. But Reagan sold the nation a bag of goods.

We can finally see clearly the failed results of this three-decade experiment in laissez faire capitalism. It has nearly destroyed the middle class in this country, greatly widened the gap between the super rich and everybody else, destabilized vital sectors of our society, and made the United States a laughingstock abroad.

Today, we have the worst of both worlds. Government bailouts for the rich—naked capitalism for everybody else.

Utopia or Dystopia?

As a historian I always wondered what evidence of the free market utopia people like [conservative commentator] David Brooks (with his "ownership society") and the army of ideologies and market fundamentalists marching in lockstep out of the Cato Institute and the Heritage Foundation and the American Enterprise Institute and Grover Norquist's Americans for Tax Reform, and all the other shills and hucksters who sold this tripe to a naive public like a greasy used car salesman selling a lemon—always wondered where is their laissez-faire utopia? Are they referring to what America looked like in 1880? A time with nearly zero federal government regulations? With no child labor laws, no limits on the hours worked, no weekend or paid overtime, no minimum wages, no workers' safety regulations, no Securities and Exchange Commission, no Federal Deposit Insurance Corporation, no worker pensions or Social Security, no right to form independent labor unions, and no vote for women? Is this their laissez faire utopia that deregulation was supposed to produce?

Today, we have the worst of both worlds. Government bailouts for the rich—naked capitalism for everybody else. This whole mess could have been avoided if the generation that followed the New Deal had the common sense and decency to understand that you cannot turn over capitalism to the capitalists. Greedy individuals will always figure out clever new ways to make their own piles of money at the expense of their fellow citizens and at the expense of their nation's well-being. Whether it's the Savings and Loan scandal of the 1980s or the Dot.com bubble of the 1990s or the Enron collapse or the mortgage meltdown—it's always the same old story. They pass on the wreckage to the taxpayer as they always do. It's time to put to rest once and for all the Big Lie that deregulation and privatization of government institutions will bring the nation anything other than calamity after calamity.

10

Military Spending Is a Form of Socialism Favored by Conservatives

Michael Lind

Michael Lind is policy director of the Economic Growth Program at the New America Foundation.

Although conservative Republicans have long denounced excessive government spending, they have been more than willing to accept government funding for the military. In essence, conservatives support a socialist military system, using government funds to stimulate business and create jobs. It has been easy for Republicans to support this spending following the terrorist attacks of September 11, 2001, noting that terrorism is an imminent threat to the United States. Some conservatives have even suggested that money devoted to other social programs such as Social Security should be cut to expand military spending. Unfortunately, this socialist-style focus on military spending is vulnerable to overextension. With the military bogged down in overseas wars, the United States finds itself in the same position as the overextended Soviet Union at the end of the 1980s.

When American conservatives denounce Keynesianism and socialism, it is difficult not to detect a note of jealous resentment on their part.[1] After all, since [President

1. Keynesianism, based on the work of English economist John Maynard Keynes, emphasizes an active role for the government in economic policy.

Ronald] Reagan, the American right has made Keynesian fiscal policy and the socialization of American industry its own specialty. Conservatives are rhetorical libertarians but operational Keynesians, when they are not operational socialists—military socialists.

The old Republican Party [aka the GOP] of [US senator] Robert Taft and [former president] Dwight Eisenhower was a fiscally conservative party of Northeasterners and Midwesterners who favored balanced budgets and viewed foreign wars and military spending with suspicion; recall Eisenhower's warning about the "military-industrial complex." The Republican Party of Ronald Reagan and his successors is based in the Southern and Western "Gun Belt," whose economy of military contracting and subsidized agriculture and energy was largely created by New Deal Democrats in World War II and the Cold War. The Republican Party seeks a permanent alliance with the Wall Street financial industry, which, however, flirts with neoliberal Democrats like [former president] Bill Clinton and [then president-elect] Barack Obama.

Both the Wall Street and the red state wings of the GOP depend on right-wing Keynesianism and right-wing socialism, in different forms. Right-wing Keynesianism for Wall Street consists of low interest rates that stimulate speculation and encourage inflation of the assets of the rich, like stocks and bonds. Right-wing socialism for Wall Street consists of "too big to fail" policies, which guarantee that over-leveraged financiers can keep their profits, while any losses will be socialized and paid for by the public.

Military Socialism

If the Wall Street wing of the GOP is factored out, the red-state Republican economy is the military-industrial complex— or, to be more specific, the agro-energy-military-industrial complex. As the political heirs of the right-wing Southern Democrats of the 1940s and 1950s, today's red-state Republicans have inherited the old Southern Democratic trick of combining denunciations of big government with support for federal government spending that benefits their constituents. Those constituents include not only well-paid military contractors, who for all practical purposes are government bureaucrats in a socialist economy, but also ordinary men and women in the ranks, where conservative white Southerners are over-represented.

As long as they are out of power, Republicans theatrically pose as fiscally conservative enemies of big government.

If you are a right-wing white Southern Republican, you can spend your entire life as a ward of the state. You can serve in the socialist economy of the military and then, as a retired officer, you can go to work for a semi-socialist major defense contractor. Both in your active-duty career, your career in the pseudo-private defense contractor sector and your retirement, you will be one of the privileged Americans who enjoys a system of socialized, single-payer healthcare—the Veterans Administration. And throughout your career as a state functionary in the socialist military sector, you can grumble about big government and denounce liberals who don't understand private enterprise. If this is Orwellian Doublethink [referring to George Orwell's novel *1984*], it is no different from that of progressives who vote for candidates who promise a new New Deal and then attack middle-class entitlements, govern on behalf of Wall Street and support multinationals that seek to offshore even more industrial jobs.

Indeed, while progressives talk endlessly about protecting American industry, conservatives actually do it—as long as the industry is military. As Floyd Norris pointed out in a story for the *New York Times*, between 2000 [and] 2009, military manufacturing increased by nearly 125 percent, while civilian manufacturing contracted by roughly 25 percent. The military, which was responsible for only 3 percent of durable goods orders in 2000, grew to account for 8 percent in 2008, before the crash.

Military Keynesianism includes infrastructure spending. To be sure, the infrastructure is in countries that the U.S. has bombed into chaos like Iraq and Afghanistan, but building foreign infrastructure generates contracts for American firms like Halliburton. Conspiracy theorists to the contrary, the Iraq and Afghan wars were motivated by misguided conservative strategy, not by rewards to contractors, but those rewards are real nonetheless.

Few conservative Republicans confess to their policy of military Keynesianism. As long as they are out of power, Republicans theatrically pose as fiscally conservative enemies of big government. If the GOP recaptured Congress or the presidency, however, [libertarian representative] Ron Paul would be locked in the attic again and [Representative] Paul Ryan's plans for downsizing the federal government would be shelved in a locked cabinet in one of those secret government warehouses depicted in *The X-Files* while even more money was shoveled at the Pentagon.

Justifying Military Spending

Martin Feldstein has given the game away. Feldstein, now a professor at Harvard, was the chairman of President Reagan's Council of Economic Advisers. For the last few years, he has been campaigning to raise defense spending to 6 percent of GDP [gross domestic product] a year (it is now 4.7 percent of GDP and reached a low of 3.0 percent in 1999–2000, after the Cold War and before 9/11). In his articles and Op-Eds, Feldstein makes minimal and unconvincing attempts to justify defense spending in terms of actual threats—jihadists, Iran, North Korea, Russia, China, whatever. It is clear that he is chiefly interested in military Keynesianism for its macroeconomic results.

In December 2008, Feldstein called for a massive Keynesian stimulus in the form of defense spending. He denounced fiscal conservatives who called for cutting spending during the recession:

> That logic is exactly backwards. As President-elect Barack Obama and his economic advisers recognize, countering a deep economic recession requires an increase in government spending to offset the sharp decline in consumer outlays and business investment that is now under way. Without that rise in government spending, the economic downturn would be deeper and longer. Although tax cuts for individuals and businesses can help, government spending will have to do the heavy lifting. That's why the Obama team will propose a package of about $300 billion a year in additional federal government outlays and grants to states and local governments.
>
> A temporary rise in DOD [US Department of Defense] spending on supplies, equipment and manpower should be a significant part of that increase in overall government outlays. The same applies to the Department of Homeland Security, to the FBI and to other parts of the national intelligence community. . . .
>
> A 10% increase in defense outlays for procurement and for research would contribute about $20 billion a year to the overall stimulus budget. A 5% rise in spending on operations and maintenance would add an additional $10 billion. That spending could create about 300,000 additional jobs. And raising the military's annual recruitment goal by 15% would provide jobs for an additional 30,000 young men and women in the first year. . . .
>
> Military procurement has the further advantage that almost all of the equipment and supplies that the military buys are made in the United States, creating demand and jobs here at home.

Even before the Great Recession began, Feldstein was campaigning for defense spending at levels near those of the Cold

War. In an essay for *Foreign Affairs* in 2007, Feldstein wrote: "Defense spending rose rapidly during the presidency of Ronald Reagan, rising to 6 percent of GDP by 1986—a trend that helped to bring about the collapse of the Soviet Union ... [I]t is useful to consider the 6 percent target achieved during the Reagan years as a spending target."

Promoting War Socialism

An obvious question is: Why stop with the Cold War? Most economists agree that U.S. military spending during World War II pulled the U.S. out of the Great Depression. In 1944, mostly military federal spending was 37.8 percent of GDP. If military spending works such wonders, why not devote 40 percent of the economy to it, and not just 6? If military Keynesianism is considered such a success by conservatives, they can hardly balk at what the Prussian military, during World War I, called "war socialism."

The logic of military Keynesianism may explain why the same conservatives who denounce allegedly wasteful civilian stimulus spending are silent about the cost overruns in the military sector. R.L. Schreadley, a retired Navy commander, asks:

> Is it credible to spend a billion dollars for one destroyer? Fifteen billion (or more) for an aircraft carrier? Multimillions for one fighter plane? No, it is not. Nor is it credible for the sea service to have two or more admirals for every ship in the fleet.

From the perspective of military Keynesianism, such costs appear to be acceptable if they stimulate the economy and provide contracts or employment for Republican voters and donors. The fact that healthcare costs have been growing faster than the economy as a whole is treated as cause for alarm. And yet here is Feldstein in 2006, calling for defense spending to rise faster than economic growth: "Increasing defense spending at a faster rate than the rate of GDP growth requires raising the share of GDP devoted to defense."

The U.S. Economy increasingly resembles the dual economy of the Soviet Union, with an overfunded military sector and a chronically weak, dysfunctional civilian sector.

In that same speech at West Point, Feldstein told a largely military audience that the money for military Keynesianism could come from cuts in Social Security and Medicare programs for elderly Americans:

The final hurdle to increased defense spending will be the effect of the population aging on the cost of Social Security and Medicare . . . That's one more good reason, in my judgment, to focus on transforming the current pure tax-financed, pay-as-you-go systems for financing Social Security and Medicare to a mixed system that combines a tax-financed basic program with individual investment-based accounts in a way that can avoid that tax increase.

Undoubtedly, many of the military personnel in Feldstein's audience nodded in agreement. The soldiers, after all, have generous military pensions and the Veterans Administration to provide their socialized healthcare in their old age.

An Overfunded Military

The U.S. economy increasingly resembles the dual economy of the Soviet Union, with an overfunded military sector and a chronically weak, dysfunctional civilian sector. Like the Soviet Union in its decline, we are bogged down in an unwinnable conflict in Afghanistan. The Soviet system was supported to the end, however, by Soviet military and intelligence personnel and defense factory workers and managers. Their equivalents exist in America. Conservatives are not being irrational when they ignore the civilian economy while fostering the military economy that provides orders and jobs to many of their constituents. Theirs is the logic of Soviet-style conservatism.

"Watch what we say, not what we do," Richard Nixon's Attorney General John Mitchell famously remarked. Out of power, the Republican Party preaches Ron Paul–style libertarianism. In power, the party practices Martin Feldstein–style military Keynesianism and military socialism—and [former treasury secretary] Hank Paulson–style financial sector Keynesianism and socialism.

11

Socialism Does Not Benefit the Poor

Kel Kelly

Kel Kelly is a Wall Street trader and the director of a Fortune 500 management consulting firm.

Although there are poor people in the United States, few are as poverty stricken as the poor in noncapitalist countries. The economically hard-pressed in America, for instance, have televisions, cars, homes, and running water. Even those who are defined as poor in the United States seldom remain poor for long. Unfortunately, government solutions to poverty only create more problems. By setting a minimum wage, for instance, the federal government guarantees that companies will hire fewer employees. Likewise, when government redistributes income, taking money from the wealthy and giving it to the poor, the wealthy have less money to invest, which means that fewer jobs will be created. The only real solution to poverty is to deregulate the minimum wage laws and to discontinue public employment programs sponsored by the government.

When we hear of the poor, we envision a massive group of people without food and shelter. In reality, most of the poor in capitalistic countries such as the United States are not in such a state. Data from a recent census reveals that of the official "poor":

Kel Kelly, *The Case for Legalizing Capitalism*, Auburn, AL: Ludwig von Mises Institute, 2010, pp. 313–323. Copyright © 2010 by Kel Kelly. All rights reserved. Reproduced by permission.

- 76 percent have air conditioning.

- 66 percent have more than two rooms of living space per person.

- 97 percent own at least one color television.

- 62 percent have either cable or satellite television.

- Almost 75 percent of households own a car (30 percent own two or more).

- 73 percent own microwave ovens.

- More than 50 percent have stereos.

- 33 percent have automatic dishwashers.

- 99 percent have refrigerators.

- Virtually none lack running water or flushing toilets.

- 46 percent own their own home, the average of which is a three bedroom house with 1.5 baths, that has a carport and porch or patio, and the average value of which is 70 percent of the median American home.

If we observe our presumably poorest citizens on our public transportation systems we see that they have cell phones, adequate clothing, personal audio devices, and are generally clean and free of disease and deformities. They also have the comfort of using a heated and air-conditioned transportation car that has carpet and flat-panel televisions for their amusement (paid for primarily by the wealthy, of course).

The Wealthy Poor vs. the Desolate Poor

If you were to compare these American poor to the poor in Bolivia, Honduras, Cambodia, or India (or even to many of the poor in Mexico, Romania, Thailand, and Russia), you would see a stark difference. The poor in these countries often literally live in open-air huts with large leaves for roofs and stacked bricks that serve as a shared stove for multiple families. For the poor of the third-world countries, there is, for the most part, no money, no exchange of goods—just basic survival by subsistence farming or by hunting or fishing for food. To these people, American street sweepers and factory workers live a life of luxury.

The difference between the "wealthy poor" in capitalist countries and the "deprived and desolate poor" in noncapitalist countries is no coincidence. The freedom that exists in capitalistic countries results in more invested capital per worker. This means that workers can produce far more wealth for themselves and for the rest of society. In noncapitalist countries today (and in the days before capitalism first appeared) poverty really means that no work is available; there is no means by which to improve one's state of being, or even to maintain it.

Under capitalism, as we see, there is almost no question of poverty existing in this sense. Anyone who is not mentally or physically disabled can perform work and earn an income if they choose (except when prevented by the setting of minimum wages by government). Today, any poverty in the world is caused by an absence of capitalism, not the existence of capitalism.

Though the poor in this country have continuously seen their standard of living rise by capitalism, anticapitalists continually point to the poor as evidence of a need for wealth redistribution (i.e., less capitalism), just because the poor earn less than do the rich. But there will always be a bottom 10 percent or 20 percent of the population in income in any society no matter how wealthy we all become. Thus, politicians and socialists always have a group to point to that are always in need of "assistance."

Who Are the Poor?

But even if we focus on the bottom 10 percent or 20 percent of Americans, it would still be difficult to identify who the poor are, because the composition of this group changes constantly. The "disadvantaged," the group that is supposedly made poor by the rich, are not a static, defined group. A study by Michael Cox and Richard Alm of the Federal Reserve Bank of Dallas showed that of the bottom fifth of income earners in 1975, only 5 percent were still poor 16 years later. Less than 1 percent remained in the bottom fifth for the entire 16 years. Thirty percent rose from the bottom fifth to the top fifth. In sum, few people remain at subsistence level. There are ways out of poverty for most.

Socialists make it appear as though there are many more poor people than there really are.

Not to diminish the pains and difficulties of poverty, but in terms of the ability to achieve an absolute level of health and strength, the "poor" are usually in the same shape as the average person. Poor children take in virtually the same amount of protein, vitamins, and minerals as middle-class children; and they actually consume more meat. Most poor children grow to be larger, stronger, and healthier than the average WWII soldier. Though some poor families have temporary challenges with hunger, 89 percent of the poor report that their families have "enough" to eat; only 2 percent say they "often" do not have enough food.

Further, the poor are not as poor as government statistics intentionally misrepresent. For example, the ratio of "incomes"—the primary measurement used by government—of the top fifth to the bottom fifth of income earners is 15 to 1, but the ratio of their consumption is 4 to 1. This is because the poor usually have access to money that does not fall under taxable income, including government handouts. Their assets and wealth are not considered at all. The census bureau previously stated that people it deems "poor" typically spend $2.24 for every $1.00 in (government) reported income.

Though there are indeed people who are in dire straits and need immediate help, most of the people we generally call "poor" are not as poor as anticapitalists make them out to be. Depending on whom they are compared to, the poor can appear to be outright rich. Socialists make it appear as though there are many more poor people than there really are, so as to justify stealing more money from the rich to try and "equal out" society. When we speak of the poor, we should only speak of those who are physically unable to work and provide for themselves, not the entire bottom 20 percent of income earners who represent tens of millions of people.

Minimum Wage's Negative Impact

The minimum wage raises labor costs to the point where companies cannot afford to hire all the workers they previously did, since they have a limited amount of funds available with which to hire workers.

Even ACORN [Association of Community Organizations for Reform Now], the organization that claims to help the poor by, among other means, promoting a "living wage," learned this firsthand. ACORN sued the state of California in 1995 for exemption from state labor laws, in order to avoid having to pay the minimum wage to its own employees. The organization argued before the court that "the more that ACORN must pay each individual outreach worker—either because of minimum wage or overtime requirements—the fewer outreach workers it will be able to hire." (As a comparable example, esteemed minimum-wage advocate Nancy Pelosi [California congresswoman and then-Speaker of the US House of Representatives] also refused to pay minimum wage to her own workers.)

But besides the fact that the minimum wage cannot truly help low-skilled workers earn higher salaries, it's not needed in order for them to do so anyway. Low-end wages, just like high-end wages, will increase through time as increased capital accumulation brings about increased productivity, and especially as workers improve their skills. For example, wage rates for minimum-wage employees grew at more than five times the rate for those earning above minimum wage between 1998 and 2002. Nearly 66 percent of all minimum wage employees who remain employed earn more than the minimum wage after one year of employment.

Our government has been "fighting poverty" for most of the last century. Tens of trillions of dollars have been spent. Yet success never comes.

Since most of the low-income earners are newer workers starting out and acquiring skills that will enable them to eventually earn more money, over 97 percent of all employees in the United States earn more than the minimum wage by age 30. Those who do not achieve this rate of pay do not acquire the needed skills for one reason or another; the explanation likely has to do with mental illness or personal motivation. Just about all workers can progress by remaining employed and gaining experience. But those who are forced into unemployment by the minimum wage often never get the opportunity.

And contrary to what ACORN, our politicians, and other socialists would have you believe, it is not usually the case that minimum-wage earners are single mothers raising children. The 1995 Current Population Survey showed that of all workers earning the minimum wage immediately prior to President Clinton's 1996 increase of that wage, 37.6 percent were teenagers living with their parents, 17.1 percent were single adults living by themselves, and 21.5 percent were adults married to a spouse who was also employed. Only 5.5 percent of workers earning minimum wage were single parents, and only 7.8 percent were married but still the sole family wage earner.

The Failure of Antipoverty Schemes

Our government has been "fighting poverty" for most of the last century. Tens of trillions of dollars have been spent. Yet success never comes. When it becomes apparent that "poverty" is not being eradicated, our politicians throw yet more money at the supposed problem. The increased money comes from our increased taxes (including the inflation tax).

Original tax rates in this country were 0 percent. The first official income tax appeared in 1913 with the passing of the Sixteenth Amendment. It was a rate of 0.4 percent—a rate that Congress deemed "fair." The original marginal tax rate on the super rich was 7 percent. It eventually reached a peacetime high of 92 percent (Sweden reached an unbelievable 102%). Once our effective tax rates reach 100 percent, we will effectively be a communist country. Year by year, working persons have had to pay a higher proportion of their incomes for their own compulsory "insurance," or to support other people.

If Americans are fully employed and earning continually increasing wages, who needs the thousands of welfare bureaucrats in Washington?

But year by year there are still more people in need of government support. This is partially because as more people understand that incomes can be had without working for them, more people position themselves as poor so that they can receive benefits. No matter how much money is thrown at the problem, there will always be both the government-defined poor as well as the natural nondisability poor; there will always be people who choose not to better themselves, due to various psychological or mental desires to remain in their current state.

Yet any attempt to equalize people by redistributing wealth must result in a destruction of capital and of the ability to create jobs and prosperity, and thus reduced incomes. Even Leonid Brezhnev, First Secretary of the Soviet Communist Party, stated that "One can only distribute and consume what has been produced; this is an elementary truth." What he failed to learn, as history shows, was that only the protection of private property and free markets can bring about the co-ordination of people and physical resources in a way that increases the production of wealth, while government economic planning and forced redistribution reduces production.

A Political Investment in Poverty

But besides the fact that so-called poverty will never be eliminated simply because at least one person will always be poorer than all others, politicians have a vested interest in preventing the alleviation of poverty. If Americans are fully employed and earning continually increasing wages, who needs the thousands of welfare bureaucrats in Washington? Though socialists believe that these bureaucrats (at least the Democrats) are truly benevolent individuals concerned about the well-being of others, in reality they are there to gain power, live off of taxpayer money, and advance their careers. Why else, for example, would Congress vote to repeatedly give itself wage increases—along with lifetime pensions in the millions—that far outpace the consumer price index and the wages of workers?

Thus, politicians will always claim that masses of poor people need their assistance. This is why they continually redefine poverty and raise the income threshold for the "poverty line." In this way they can instantly have more poor people who need help from more taxpayer money and more bureaucrats. Our welfare and redistribution system sustains an industry of tens of millions of both public and private "aid" workers. Actual facts and outcomes of this industry's work demonstrate that its goal is not to eliminate poverty, but to expand government dependence through increased taxing, spending, and regulation.

Why do voters not see that the welfare policies of the last hundred years have failed to alleviate "poverty" and that something different should be done? Many do, but too many other people benefit (or so they think) from the current system by having money redistributed to them; they thus keep voting for it. Also, many of the people are socialists with socialist ideals detached from reality. I suppose the rest of the well-intentioned voters are simply naïve.

Redistributing wealth from the rich to the poor only reduces the wealth of both groups, but particularly of the poor.

Real Solutions to Poverty

Very few people examine why the poor are poor. We generally give our and others' money to "the poor" because we blindly believe that they can't help the situation they're in and that they would otherwise starve or freeze to death. But if we really delve into their past and look at the decisions they have made, we would find that most of the ongoing poor are poor largely because they have, through their own actions and inactions, chosen to be. Many people think it is immoral to "judge" them and to consider the notion that they might have brought it on themselves. We don't question why we observe many of the poor visibly doing nothing day by day while we are at our offices working to support them.

Similarly, many of us workers see even coworkers who are not nearly as hard-working and who clearly just show up to collect a paycheck between nine and five without putting a lot of thought and care into their work. We don't like to admit that these work habits could be related to why these workers do not earn as much as others who work much harder.

As another example, most of us have family or extended family members who do not have much wealth because they have lived well beyond their means and have made poor personal and career decisions. We have family members that chose not to continue their education—education that is free to the poor—and chose not to work hard to have a career (granted, its not obligatory to have a "career," but it is in fact what usually brings in more money).

We ignore these things and pretend that each and every poor person achieved their current state by being held down by the exploitative actions of others. We thus vote over and over to hand over money, not mostly from ourselves, but mainly from the rich, to the poor. The more we give the poor, the more incentive they have to rely on what we give them instead of earning more for themselves, an act which would require time, effort, and hardship on their part.

The Failure of Wealth Redistribution

Redistributing wealth from the rich to the poor only reduces the wealth of both groups, but particularly of the poor. Every country that has ever made a serious attempt to equalize its citizens has gone to ruin, because forced equality reduces the incentive the rich have to invest capital and instead encourages the consumption of it, since it is likely to be taken from them. Additionally, as more and more people choose to become receivers instead of givers, there is not enough wealth being created by those who produce to support both themselves and the rest of society. The system breaks down and poverty for all arises.

Socialism and communism always falsely parade as systems of equality and liberty of all citizens, but they have always resulted in economic retrogression for all (except the rulers). Partial socialism, as we have today, has always resulted in stagnant or slowly retrogressing economic performance, as we have today.

The general public does not understand that taking money from the rich has a very real and negative economic cause and effect; they imagine some economic vacuum in which there is no real change in the amount of capital per worker and their corresponding wages. They think that government, not businesses, creates wealth and provides for them. They see government as a spender, not as the taker that it is.

As Ludwig von Mises stated, "Spending and unbalanced budgets are merely synonyms for capital consumption." The only real way to improve the lot of the poor is to replace their payments from government with payments from companies, in the form of wages.

Jobs for Everyone

The first and easiest step to increase the incomes of the poor would be to eliminate all laws that fix the price of labor above the market price. This alone would create full employment. The average poor family with children is supported by only 800 hours of work each year. This is equivalent to 16 hours of work per week. If the average poor family was able to increase the hours worked to 2,000 hours each year (i.e., one adult family member working a full 40 hour week), nearly 75 percent of poor children would be lifted out of poverty. This could be achieved by eliminating labor laws that require potential employers to pay workers wages higher than the market price they would otherwise pay.

The only possible way to help the poor is to provide jobs that are profitable.

If poor workers were able (and willing) to work as many hours as a lot of middle- and upper-class workers do—50, 60, or even 70 hours per week—they could afford to live on minimum wage and below, especially if they had few or no children (the government currently gives them the incentive to have children by paying them for each child).

The second step towards helping the poor would be to cease all redistribution payments. This would cause workers' real wages to increase because the money that was previously consumed by being redistributed through antipoverty programs would be used by companies to purchase more capital goods and pay more wages, resulting in increased productivity and thus more consumer goods, resulting in lower prices relative to wages.

This is true even if we take into account that the government might still be printing money, causing all prices to rise. In this case, all prices will rise, but the price of labor—our wages—would rise faster, because the supply of labor would not be increasing as fast as the supply of goods; in other words, inflation would not push prices of goods higher as fast as it pushes prices of wages higher.

Changes in real wages always follow changes in productivity. When real wages don't keep up with inflation (such as right now), the explanation is almost certainly that real productivity is not increasing. This is ultimately because we are consuming capital as fast or faster than we are replacing it.

Real wealth is created only through production. Thus, the only possible way to help the poor is to provide jobs that are profitable. Providing jobs without the corresponding creation of more goods—such as unprofitable, government-created "green jobs"—does not help anyone. These, and other government-created jobs involving public-works projects result mostly in the destruction of capital and wealth. The few government jobs that involve improving roads, ports, and railways do allow us to produce more goods, but these projects could be performed more cheaply and efficiently by individual firms.

Failed Government Work Programs

More importantly, government does not use market prices to determine which projects need to be undertaken when; instead, the decisions are made based on politics. The result is too much of one good or service and too little of another. This is why, for example, we have too few roads and therefore "too much traffic."

Government-works projects are usually taken on during bad economic times when unemployment is high. Politicians "create" these jobs in addition to the ones that already existed to serve the same purpose. But what is needed is not new jobs to perform inefficient, wealth-consuming work, but jobs in private industry to create real wealth. Government-works projects hire workers who, had they not been prevented from doing so by previous government regulation and intervention, would otherwise be working for individual companies and contributing to the production of real wealth.

Real-wealth-producing jobs, which contribute to increasing real wages, can come about only by allowing companies the freedom to produce as they see fit, and by allowing capital to work for us instead of being consumed in redistribution. Poverty can be solved only with profitable wage payments and lower costs of living arising from increasing productivity. As long as we are producing and as long as there are not regulations preventing employment, there will always be jobs for everyone.

12

Nationalized Education Would Be Harmful and Socialistic

Lee Cary

Lee Cary is a columnist for the American Thinker.

After socializing health care, President Barack Obama and the Democratic Congress will turn to public education. In fact, as a candidate Obama talked more about his plans for education than for health care. Nationalizing education would place America's school system under the control of the federal government, eliminating local school districts and school boards. Because federal control would eliminate local school taxes and decrease the overall tax rate, many Americans will view this change as sensible. Nationalized schools, however, will change how Americans think about democracy, advocating the redistribution of income in an attempt to achieve equality. Unless Americans want to trade local control for a national school czar, however, socialist schools are a bad idea.

After Congress passes a national health care plan, nationalizing public education will be next.

John Naisbitt, author of *Megatrends* (1988), said something to the effect that Ronald Reagan wasn't leading the (conservative) parade; he was riding the horse that was leading the parade.

Barack Obama is leading the progressive parade, and his wagon is hitched to a team of horses that includes a compliant Democrat Congress, well-funded liberal think tanks, a shill media, and the collective mindset of a progressive movement active since the early 20th Century.

The Great Depression chaos gave FDR [President Franklin Delano Roosevelt] the opportunity to dramatically alter the nation's socio-political landscape. Likewise, the implosion of the credit market in 2008 gave the Obama administration the chaos needed to cram down its progressive initiatives with breathtaking speed.

The Republicans have neither the votes nor the collective will to turn back the tide of Obama-style change that represents a mix of socialist and fascist economic policies not new to the planet, but new in their current intensity in America. The Democrats are playing hardball; the Republicans are lobbing mush pounders.

Candidate Obama's language about reforming public education was more emphatic and detailed than his discussion of health care.

Though not yet in great numbers, some who voted for Obama are now being heard to say that they didn't vote for what's happening. Those confessions illustrate their failure to do due diligence on the candidate of their choice. His intentions were clearly laid out in his campaign documents and in many of his non-primetime speeches.

When the nation was watching, he was all about hope and change, based on a delivery style that hid content vagaries. When more focused interest groups were addressed, his language foretold the sort of change he intended. Consequently, little of what's happened comes as any surprise to those who kept up with the full array of his messages. But few voters had time for that. And the old liberal media had no interest.

Socializing Education

So we come to the point where the financial markets, the auto industry and eventually the health care industry will function under the aegis [authority] of the federal government. It's clear from his campaign rhetoric what will come next— America's public education system.

Candidate Obama's language about reforming public education was more emphatic and detailed than his discussion of health care. And, making a case for nationalizing public education will attract broader support than the three previous venues (banking, autos, and health care).

President Obama will proclaim public education K–12 as too crucial to the future of the nation to be left in the hands of volunteer citizen committees, also known as School Boards and Independent School Districts. And the distribution of school financing is, Obama will say, too dependent on the varying affluence levels among the states, and within their divergent communities. All of America's youth are entitled to an equal opportunity to receive a world class education. Anything less is unfair. Equal opportunity demands equal funding. It doesn't take a crystal ball to see this coming.

Most citizens will see no inherent danger in bringing central planning to public education.

The pragmatic case for uniform public education will cite economy-of-scale advantages whereby the federal government will eliminate multiple duplications of effort in a currently over-staffed management equation where every school district constructs its own buildings, buys its own materials, hires its own staff, and manages its own curriculum to its own state's standards. Why not centralize all those processes and save time, effort and money, will be the argument. Works for Wal-Mart.

Large metropolitan school districts that are almost all dismal failures will gladly turn over their responsibility to the federal government. Most teachers and administrators will welcome the opportunity to become GS workers [government employees paid under the federal general scale] and enjoy the benefits of greater and more equitable pay, plus relocation opportunities without compensation penalties. Many will welcome the end of the politico-educational fiefdoms called school districts.

Rationalizations

Compared to the complexity of redesigning the American health care system, rationalizing the nationalizing of public education K–12 will be a snap. Most citizens will see no inherent danger in bringing central planning to public education. After all, central equals public, public equals central. So the argument will go.

Obama will claim that taxpayers will pay less for nationalized education since the increase in their federal taxes will be less than what they're now paying in local school taxes, which will go away. Lower taxes—that'll sell.

What groups will oppose this? Besides home schoolers, that is. They'll be required to meet the same certification standards as national teachers, and jump through bureaucratic hoops that'll eventually dissuade many from being their child's teacher as well as their parent.

Here's one look behind the curtain pertaining to the political philosophy that'll drive the effort to nationalize public education.

John E. Roemer, Professor of Political Science/Economics, Yale University, wrote the following in an article entitled "Socialism vs. Social Democracy as Income-Equalizing Institutions" [published in 2008 in the *Eastern Economic Journal*].

One must not confuse socialism with democracy. Democracy, as I see it, is a set of political institutions (competitive parties, contested elections, etc.), while socialism, defined here, is a property of an allocation. Thorough-going democracy may well reduce inequality, both through the redistribution of income, and through the educational investments in the population that it engenders. It is much less clear what the relationship between democracy and socialism is. My own view is that democracy tends to eliminate inequality of opportunity—this statement must be qualified—but there is little reason to believe it will eliminate (Marxian) [after German philosopher Karl Marx] exploitation—and, perhaps, even for those who consider themselves socialists, this should not much matter. . . .

Granted that the socialist allocation, given the distribution of skills in the United States today, would bring with it a relatively high degree of income inequality, but under socialism, that distribution of skills would change. If socialism brings the culture and politics that its advocates claim, the skill distribution would become more equal, and so, if one views the problem dynamically, then socialism over time would probably be more income-egalitarian than capitalism with a 31 percent tax rate. Indeed, the high skewness of the distribution of skills in the US is in large part due to inequality of educational opportunity. I sympathize with this response; however, it is only an acceptable one if we broaden the definition of socialism to include a mechanism for the development of human capital in the population (presumably, some kind of equal-opportunity educational system). . . .

My rhetorical point is that socialism (distribution of output in proportion to the value of labor performed) is not enough. Equalizing opportunities for the realization of skills from natural talents—however that be further articulated—must be of central importance to inequality-averse socialists today. . . .

To press the point even further: equality of opportunity may not be enough. Imagine that the distribution of innate talents is such that an equal-opportunity educational system would still engender a great deal of income inequality. Many would still advocate redistributive taxation, justifiable under the Rawlsian [after political philosopher John Rawls] construal that the distribution of talents is morally arbitrary.

The Coming of School Czars

And there it is. Federal control over "some kind of equal opportunity educational system" might lead to more equal development of innate skills, but it would need to be supplemented by a redistributive tax system that spreads the wealth to accompany an equalization of skills. A twofer, as it were.

Unless the nation pushes back against the trend, local communities will lose control over their neighborhood schools and a Beltway [Washington, D.C.,] *School Czar* will be in our future.

13

Socialist Policies Are Necessary to Save Public Education

Jerry White

Jerry White is an American political activist and cofounder of Survivor Corps, a global network advocating for survivors of war and conflict.

Although a number of commentators have labeled President Barack Obama a socialist, his public education policies are a continuation of conservative policies toward schools. Since President Ronald Reagan's administration during the 1980s, politicians have been reducing funds for public education and promoting privatized schools. This trend ignores the ideology of the nation's Founding Fathers, who believed that an educated public promoted democracy and equality. Because neither political party supports these ideas today, the public school system is being dismantled. The only way to reverse this trend is to support socialist policies, redistributing wealth to support an education system that serves all Americans.

The [President Barack] Obama administration is spearheading an unprecedented assault on public education in the United States. While providing trillions of dollars to Wall Street, Obama has starved states and local governments of funding and pressed them to address their soaring budget deficits by closing public schools and opening semi-private charter schools.

In Michigan and other states, school districts are slashing jobs and eliminating essential services such as student transportation. The school week in Hawaii has been reduced to four days due to teacher furloughs. The cutbacks have been extended to higher education as well, with California leading the way by imposing a 32 percent tuition increase.

What little federal funding the Obama administration has made available—a meager $4 billion in its "Race to the Top" program—is contingent on school districts' dropping restrictions on the expansion of charter schools and tying school funding and teachers' pay to standardized test scores.

The catastrophe facing the public schools is the culmination of three decades of attacks on education, which has coincided with a general assault on the social position and democratic rights of the working class. The assault began in earnest in the 1980s with Reagan, who halved the federal share of education funding. It continued with [President Bill] Clinton's promotion of charter schools and "school choice" in the 1990s and [President George W.] Bush's "No Child Left Behind Act," co-sponsored by Democratic Senator Edward Kennedy.

Quality education is fast becoming a privilege of the few, not the right of all.

Privatizing Public Schools

It has no doubt come as a shock to many teachers and supporters of public education that the current administration, elected by appealing to popular sentiment for an end to social reaction and exploiting the belief that an African-American president would be more sympathetic to working people, has become the vehicle for an even more ruthless attack on the public schools. However, the assault on education is of a piece with all of Obama's policies, including the escalation of war and the further enrichment of the financial aristocracy.

The policies of Obama and his education secretary, Arne Duncan, represent a repudiation of the basic democratic principle that all children, regardless of their socio-economic background, have the right to a free, quality education. The administration is spearheading the transformation of education into a largely privatized system, with government subsidies provided to charter schools which are designed to educate only a fraction of working class youth. The rest are condemned to schools that are more like holding pens than centers of learning.

Quality education is fast becoming a privilege of the few, not the right of all.

Detroit, the poorest major city in the US, has become a focal point of this attack. Working closely with the Obama administration as well as the American Federation of Teachers and its Detroit local, the school district's state-appointed "emergency financial director" has just imposed a contract that forces each teacher to "loan" the district $10,000 from their pay over the next two years. The contract will accelerate the closing of so-called "failing schools" and the firing of experienced teachers, combined with the establishment of "priority schools" for a select section of students.

An educated populace, the American revolutionaries believed, was the only means to prevent tyranny and oppression.

The conditions of mass unemployment in the former center of world auto production, compounded by aged and inadequately maintained school buildings and a shameful dearth of basic tools such as books, computers, labs, etc., have led to falling test scores and plummeting graduation rates. Far from seeking to reverse this disaster, the politicians and school administrators have utilized the crisis to scapegoat the teachers and undermine public confidence in the public school system.

This is a deliberate class policy. The American ruling elite, dominated by a fabulously rich and corrupt financial oligarchy, has no intention of investing money to educate large sections of working class youth who face a future of unemployment or poverty-level wages.

The most critical measure of the health of a society is the value it places and resources it dedicates to raising the cultural and intellectual level of the next generation. The state of public education in the US is an indictment of capitalist society.

Social Equality and Education

The establishment of public schools in the US was the product of the revolutionary upheavals of the 18th and 19th centuries against social inequality and oppression. The greatest leaders of the American Revolution believed that every individual had innate potential, which could be realized if he was provided with the means to gain knowledge and training. Thomas Jefferson in 1779 proposed a bill for the "more general diffusion of knowledge." It called for the establishment of free public schools. This, he said, would "bring into action that mass of talents which lies buried in poverty in every country for want of the means of development...."

An educated populace, the American revolutionaries believed, was the only means to prevent tyranny and oppression. The public cost for establishing a system of free schools, Jefferson said, would be "not more than the thousandth part of what will be paid to kings, priests and nobles who will rise up among us if we leave the people in ignorance."

The destruction of public education is a profound expression of the terminal crisis of democracy in the US.

The fighters for public education—from the "father of the common school" Horace Mann, the abolitionist Thaddeus Stevens and the philosopher John Dewey to the early working class and socialist leaders and the pioneers of the civil rights movement—were driven by a profound belief that every child—whether a former slave, child laborer or working class immigrant—should and could be educated, and that the continued existence of democracy depended on it.

Today, the American corporate and political establishment has repudiated this egalitarian conception. In its eyes, the cost of educating tens of millions of working class youth—especially in the inner cities—is an intolerable infringement on its wealth. This misanthropic class policy is camouflaged by invocations to "individual responsibility." As Obama—who has made his career and his millions by lending his services to the rich and powerful—has repeatedly declared, poverty and decaying schools are "no excuse for failure."

The assault on public education is the outcome of the growth of social inequality in America, which, in turn, is the most perverse expression of the decay of American and world capitalism. The immense and growing chasm between the top 1 percent of society and the broad mass of the population is incompatible with democracy. The destruction of public education is a profound expression of the terminal crisis of democracy in the US.

The Crisis of Public Education

The US financial aristocracy, parasitic and criminal in its social and economic essence, exercises a de facto dictatorship, dominating both parties and every political institution. It is organically hostile to democratic principles.

The impact of decades of political reaction, the collapse of the old labor movement and the semi-criminalization of socialist politics and thought have blighted intellectual and cultural life. The critical and oppositionist liberal intelligentsia of the past has long since ceased to exist. On basic issues of policy, the Democratic and Republican parties have become virtually indistinguishable, as exemplified by the Obama administration's continuation of the militarist and pro-corporate policies of the Bush administration.

No section of the political establishment is committed to the defense of democratic rights, including the right to a decent education.

As for the unions, they have become corporatist partners in the destruction of the living standards of social conditions of the working class. The American Federation of Teachers and National Education Association have signed on to the anti-education and anti-teacher policies of the corporate elite and the government, hoping thereby to secure the salaries and perks of the union executives.

The crisis of public education in the US is deeply rooted in the crisis of the existing economic and political system. The fight to defend education is a political and revolutionary question.

Public education can be defended only through the struggle for socialism. This means the mobilization of the working class to break the grip of the financial aristocracy and establish the democratic control of working people over economic and political life. This is the only way to allocate the wealth produced by the working class and utilize the immense technological and human resources that already exist to improve the schools and raise the economic and cultural level of the people, instead of their being plundered for the benefit of a modern-day aristocracy.

The fight of teachers, students and parents to defend public education is a political struggle against the Obama administration, the Democrats and Republicans, and the capitalist system, which they defend.

14

Socialism Is Evil

Jackie Durkee

Jackie Durkee writes for her blog Faithful in Prayer.

In the 1950s, the Soviet leader Nikita Khruschev threatened that, even without a Russian military attack, socialism gradually would be implemented in the United States, ultimately leading to communism. In fact, socialism has been attempting to undermine core American values for at least 100 years. From a Catholic perspective, all men and women should live by essential principles, including a commitment to family and community. Socialism rejects these principles and seeks to eliminate personal liberty, while pretending to advocate for social justice; for this reason, Christians must remain vigilant.

Quote from Nikita Khruschev:

> We will take America without firing a shot. . . . We will BURY YOU! We can't expect the American People to jump from Capitalism to Communism, but we can assist their elected leaders in giving them small doses of Socialism, until they awaken one day to find that they have Communism. We do not have to invade the United States; we will destroy you from within.

> (From an address to Western Ambassadors at the Polish embassy in Moscow on November 18, 1956)

I don't know that it is Russia destroying us, but it is at least socialism that is destroying the United States. Socialism is an evil in this world. It seeks to deprive us of our God-given rights and it has been infiltrating our society little by little for over 100 years. I believe many Americans have finally woken up, but there are still too many who are still sleeping or walking around with blinders on. One of the ways it tries to accomplish its infiltration is through social justice and this has confused many Catholics because social justice is one of the things taught in the church. However the social justice taught by Socialism is not the same thing as the social justice taught in the Catholic Church.

The principles of Catholic Social teachings [have their] foundations laid by Pope Leo XIII's 1891 encyclical letter entitled "Rerum Novarum," which is subtitled "On Capital and Labor". Pope Leo set out the Catholic Church's response to the social instability and labor conflict that had risen in the wake of industrialization and that had led to the rise of socialism.

Some of the principles include:

Life and Dignity of the Human Person

The Church teaches that human life is sacred and that the dignity of the human person is the foundation of a moral vision for society. This belief is the foundation of all the principles of our social teaching.

Call to Family, Community, and Participation

The person is not only sacred but also social. How we organize our society—in economics and politics, in law and policy—directly affects human dignity and the capacity of individuals to grow in community. Marriage and family are the central social institutions that must be supported and strengthened, not undermined. People have a right and duty to participate in society, seeking together the common good and well-being of all, especially the poor and vulnerable. (Nowhere does it state that the government should do it.)

Rights and Responsibilities

Human dignity can be protected and a healthy community can be achieved only if human rights are protected and responsibilities are met. We have a duty to one another, to our families, and to the larger society.

Option for the Poor and Vulnerable

A basic moral test is how our most vulnerable members are faring. In a society marred by deepening divisions between rich and poor, our tradition recalls the story of the Last Judgment (Matthew 25:31-46) and instructs us to put the needs of the poor and vulnerable first. (Not by the government, but by Christians.)

The Dignity of Work and the Rights of Workers

Work is more than a way to make a living; it is a form of continuing participation in God's creation. If the dignity of work is to be protected, then the basic rights of workers must be respected—the right to productive work, to decent and fair wages, to private property and to economic initiative.

Socialism is evil and goes against the liberty of man.

Solidarity

We are one human family whatever our national, racial, ethnic, economic, and ideological differences. We are our brothers' and sisters' keepers, wherever they may be. Loving our neighbor has global dimensions in a shrinking world. Our love for all our sisters and brothers demands that we promote peace in a world surrounded by violence and conflict.

Subsidiarity

Higher levels of community, such as the government, should only perform functions not better performed by lower levels of community, such as families and charities. The church teaches that the wealthy have an obligation to the poor, but that this is a PERSONAL DUTY, not something the government should mandate or control. The obligation should be personal in nature (i.e., get involved), whereas government programs separate the giver from the receiver. The church discourages class welfare and contends that envy of the rich is a violation of the 9th commandment.

Care for God's Creation

We show our respect for the Creator by our stewardship of creation. Care for the earth is not just an Earth Day slogan; it is a requirement of our faith. We are called to protect people and the planet, living our faith in relationship with all of God's creation. This environmental challenge has fundamental, moral and ethical dimensions that cannot be ignored. *(It is not talking about global warming and carbon emissions— smart people now know that is all bogus.)*

The Catholic Church as well as all churches know that socialism is evil and goes against the liberty of man. But Christians need to be vigilant and aware that it walks around the United States as a wolf in lamb's clothing parading itself as social justice when in actuality it is government wanting to control every aspect of people's lives.

15

Socialism Would Benefit Humankind

G.A. Cohen

G.A. Cohen (1941–2009) was Chichele Professor of Social and Political Theory at Oxford University.

The principles at work during a typical camping trip illustrate the virtues of socialism. When most people go camping, they work together in the spirit of cooperation. Food and labor are shared, with each person contributing his or her individual talents. Most people would find the thought of everyone bartering and bargaining over labor and resources during a camping trip distasteful. While applying socialist principles to everyday life may be more complicated than applying them to a camping trip, they are nonetheless illustrative. Socialist principles reject the selfishness of capitalism, working to build community and equality. By promoting these principles, socialism advances human development, pushing it beyond self-interest.

You and I and a whole bunch of other people go on a camping trip. There is no hierarchy among us, our common aim is that each of us should have a good time, doing, so far as possible, the things that he or she likes best (some of those things we do together, others we do separately). We have facilities with which to carry out our enterprise: we have, for example, pots and pans, oil, coffee, fishing rods, canoes, a soccer ball, decks of cards, and so forth. And, as is usual on camping trips, we avail ourselves of those facilities collectively: even if they are privately owned things, they are under collective control for the duration of the trip, and we have shared understandings about who is going to use them when, and under what circumstances, and why. Somebody fishes, somebody else prepares the food, and another person cooks it. People who hate cooking but enjoy washing up may do all the washing up, and so on. There are plenty of differences, but our mutual understandings, and the spirit of the enterprise, ensure that there are no inequalities to which anyone could mount a principled objection.

It is commonly true on camping trips and, for that matter, in many other non-massive contexts, that people co-operate within a common concern that, so far as is possible, everybody has a roughly similar opportunity to flourish, and also to relax, on condition that they contribute, appropriately to their capacity, to the flourishing and relaxing of others. In these contexts most people, even most anti-egalitarians, accept—indeed, take for granted—norms of equality and reciprocity. So deeply do most people take those norms for granted that no one on such trips questions them: to question them would contradict the spirit of the trip.

A Capitalist Camping Trip

You could imagine a camping trip where everybody asserts their rights over the pieces of equipment, and the talents, that they bring, and where bargaining proceeds with respect to who is going to pay what to whom to be allowed, for example, to use a knife to peel the potatoes, and how much they are going to charge others for those now peeled potatoes which they bought in an unpeeled condition from another camper, and so on. You could base a camping trip on the principles of market exchange and strictly private ownership of the required facilities.

Now, most people would hate that. Most people would be more drawn to the first kind of camping trip than to the second, primarily on grounds of fellowship, but also on grounds of efficiency. (I have in mind the inordinate transaction costs that would attend a market-style camping trip. Too much time would be spent bargaining, and looking over one's shoulder for more lucrative possibilities.) And this means that most people are drawn to the socialist ideal at least in certain restricted settings.

To reinforce this point, here are some conjectures about how most people would react in various imaginable camping scenarios:

a) Harry loves fishing, and Harry is very good at fishing. Consequently, he catches, and provides, more fish than others do. Harry says: "It's unfair, how we're running things. I should have better fish when we dine. I should have only perch, not the mix of perch and catfish that we've all been having." But his fellow campers say: "Oh, for heaven's sake, Harry, don't be such a schmuck. You sweat and strain no more than the rest of us do. So, you're very good at fishing. We don't begrudge you that special endowment, which is, quite properly, a source of satisfaction to you, but why should we reward your good fortune?"

b) Following a three-hour time-off-for-personal-exploration period, an excited Sylvia returns to the campsite and announces: "I've stumbled upon a huge apple tree, full of perfect apples." "Great," others exclaim, "now we can all have apple sauce, and apple pie, and apple strudel!" "Provided, of course," so Sylvia rejoins, "that you reduce my labour burden, and/or furnish me with more room in the tent, and/or with more bacon at breakfast." Her claim to (a kind of) ownership of the tree revolts the others.

c) The trippers are walking along a bridle path on which they discover a cache of nuts that some squirrel has abandoned. Only Leslie, who has been endowed from birth with many knacks and talents, knows how to crack them, but she wants to charge for sharing that information. The campers see no important difference between her demand and Sylvia's.

d) Morgan recognises the campsite. "Hey, this is where my father camped 30 years ago. This is where he dug a special little pond on the other side of that hill, and stocked it with specially good fish. Dad knew I might come camping here one day, and he did all that so that I could eat better when I'm here. Great. Now I can have better food than you guys have." The rest frown, or smile, at Morgan's greed.

Building Community

Of course, not everybody likes camping trips. I do not myself enjoy them much, because I'm not outdoorsy, or, at any rate, I'm not outdoorsy overnight-without-a-mattress-wise. There's a limit to the outdoorsiness to which some academics can be expected to submit: I'd rather have my socialism in the warmth of All Souls College, Oxford, than in the wet of the Catskills, and I love modern plumbing. But the question I'm asking is not: Wouldn't you like to go on a camping trip? Rather: Isn't this, the socialist way, with collective property and planned mutual giving, rather obviously the best way to run a camping trip, whether or not you actually like camping?

Socialism is humanity's attempt "to overcome and advance beyond the predatory phase of human development".

The circumstances of the camping trip are multiply special: many features distinguish it from the circumstances of life in a modern society. One may therefore not infer, from the fact that camping trips of the sort that I have described are feasible and desirable, that society-wide socialism is equally feasible and equally desirable. There are too many major differences between the contexts for that inference to carry any conviction. What we urgently need to know is precisely what are the differences that matter, and how can socialists address them? Because of its contrasts with life in the large, the camping trip model serves well as a reference point for purported demonstrations that socialism across society is not feasible and/or desirable, since it seems eminently feasible and desirable on the trip.

Two principles are realised on the trip—an egalitarian principle, and a principle of community. The egalitarian principle in question is one of radical equality of opportunity. Equality of opportunity removes obstacles to opportunity from which some people suffer and others don't, obstacles that are sometimes due to the enhanced opportunities that the more privileged people enjoy.

"Community" can mean many things, but the requirement of community that is central here is that people care about, and, where necessary and possible, care for, one another, and care that they care about one another.

Any attempt to realise the socialist ideal runs up against entrenched capitalist power and individual human selfishness. Politically serious people must take those obstacles seriously. But they are not reasons to disparage the ideal itself. I agree with Albert Einstein that socialism is humanity's attempt "to overcome and advance beyond the predatory phase of human development". Our attempt to get beyond predation has thus far failed. I do not think the right conclusion is to give up.

Organizations to Contact

The editors have compiled the following list of organizations concerned with the issues debated in this book. The descriptions are derived from materials provided by the organizations. All have publications or information available for interested readers. The list was compiled on the date of publication of the present volume; names; addresses, phone and fax numbers, and e-mail and Internet addresses may change. Be aware that many organizations take several weeks or longer to respond to inquiries, so allow as much time as possible.

American Enterprise Institute (AEI)

1150 Seventeenth St. NW, Washington, DC 20036
(202) 862-5800 • fax: (202) 862-7177
website: www.aei.org

The American Enterprise Institute is a public policy institute that sponsors research and provides commentary on a wide variety of issues, including economics, social welfare, and government tax and regulatory policies. AEI publishes the bimonthly magazine *American Enterprise* and the *AEI Newsletter*.

Brookings Institution

1775 Massachusetts Ave. NW, Washington, DC 20036
(202) 797-6000 • fax: (202) 797-6004
e-mail: brookinfo@brook.edu
website: www.brookings.edu

Founded in 1927, the Brookings Institution is a think tank that conducts research and supports education in foreign policy, economics, government, and the social sciences. The organization's publications include the quarterly *Brookings Review*, periodic *Policy Briefs*, and various books.

Cato Institute

1000 Massachusetts Ave. NW, Washington, DC   20001-5403
(202) 842-0200 • fax: (202) 842-3490
e-mail: cato@cato.org
website: www.cato.org

The Cato Institute is a nonpartisan libertarian public policy research foundation dedicated to limiting the role of government and protecting individual liberties. It publishes the quarterly magazine *Regulation*, the bimonthly *Cato Policy Report*, and numerous policy papers and articles.

Center for American Progress Action Fund

1333 H St. NW, 10th Fl., Washington, DC   20005
(202) 682-1611
e-mail: progress@americanprogressaction.org
website: www.americanprogressaction.org

The Center for American Progress Action Fund is a progressive think tank that aims to improve the lives of Americans through advocacy, grassroots organization, and partnerships with other progressive leaders. The organization publishes a number of newsletters, including the *Progress Report*, and its website hosts several policy blogs, including *The Wonk Room, Think Progress*, and *Yglesias*.

Center for a New American Dream

6930 Carroll Ave., Suite 900, Takoma Park, MD   20912
(301) 891-3683
e-mail: newdream@newdream.org
website: www.newdream.org

The Center for a New American Dream is an organization whose goal is to help Americans consume responsibly and thus protect the earth's resources and improve the quality of life for all. Its Kids and Commercialism Campaign provides information on the effects of advertising on children. The center publishes booklets and a quarterly newsletter, *Enough*.

Competitive Enterprise Institute (CEI)

1899 L St. NW, 12th Fl., Washington, DC   20036
e-mail: info@cei.org
website: www.cei.org

The Competitive Enterprise Institute is a nonprofit public policy organization dedicated to advancing the principles of free enterprise and limited government. It believes that individuals are best helped not by government intervention but by making their own choices in a free marketplace. CEI's publications include the monthly newsletter *Monthly Planet* and articles including "The Winds of Global Change: Which Way Are They Blowing?" and "The Triumph of Democratic Capitalism: The Threat of Global Governance," which are available on its website.

Democratic National Committee

430 South Capitol St. SE, Washington, DC   20003
(202) 863-8000
website: www.democrats.org

The Democratic National Committee is the principal organization governing the Democratic Party, one of the two main political parties in the United States. The organization's website includes the party platform, press releases, news articles, radio addresses, and other articles and publications.

Democratic Socialists of America (DSA)

75 Maiden Ln., Suite 505, New York, NY   10038
(212) 727-8612
e-mail: dsa@dsausa.org
website: www.dsausa.org/dsa.html

The Democratic Socialists of America is the largest socialist organization in the United States and the principal US affiliate of the Socialist International. DSA's members are building progressive movements for social change while establishing an openly socialist presence in American communities and politics.

Green Party of the United States
PO Box 57065, Washington, DC   20037
Toll-free:(866) 414-7336 • fax: (202) 319-7193
e-mail: info@gp.org
website: www.gp.org

The Green Party of the United States is a political party dedicated to environmental and social justice issues and to grassroots activism. The organization contests local as well as national elections, and its website includes the party platform, press releases, and news articles. The Green Party publishes a quarterly newspaper, the *Green Pages*, and an e-newsletter, *Greenline*.

The Heritage Foundation
214 Massachusetts Ave. NE, Washington, DC   20002-4999
Toll-free:(800) 546-2843 • fax: (202) 544-2260
e-mail: pubs@heritage.org
website: www.heritage.org

The Heritage Foundation is a conservative public policy research institute that supports the principles of free enterprise and limited government in environmental matters. Its many publications include the Heritage Backgrounder series and various position papers.

Hoover Institution
434 Galvez Mall, Stanford University
Stanford, CA   94305-6010
(650) 723-1754 • fax: (650) 723-1687
website: www.hoover.org

Founded in 1919 by future president Herbert Hoover, the Hoover Institution is a public policy research center devoted to advancing the study of politics, economics, and political economy—both domestic and foreign—as well as international affairs. It publishes the quarterly *Hoover Digest* and *Policy Review* as well as various books.

Hudson Institute

1015 Fifteenth St. NW, 6th Fl., Washington, DC 20005
(202) 974-2400 • fax: (202) 974-2410
e-mail: info@hudson.org
website: www.hudson.org

The Hudson Institute is a nonpartisan policy research organization that aims to challenge conventional thinking and help manage strategic transitions to the future through interdisciplinary and collaborative studies in defense, international relations, economics, culture, science, technology, and law.

Libertarian Party

2600 Virginia Ave. NW, Suite 200, Washington, DC 20037
(202) 333-0008 • fax: (202) 333-0072
e-mail: info@lp.org
website: www.lp.org

The Libertarian Party is an American political party dedicated to individual liberty, free enterprise, and personal responsibility. The organization's website includes the party platform, news updates, and other information about the party.

Progressive Policy Institute

1301 Connecticut Ave. NW, Suite 450, Washington, DC 20036
(202) 525-3926 • fax: (202) 525-3941
website: www.ppionline.org

The Progressive Policy Institute is a public policy research organization that strives to develop alternatives to the traditional debate between liberals and conservatives. It advocates economic policies designed to stimulate broad upward mobility and social policies designed to liberate the poor from poverty and dependence. The institute's publications include the book *Building the Bridge: 10 Big Ideas to Transform America.*

Rand Corporation

1776 Main St., Santa Monica, CA   90401-3208
(310) 393-0411 • fax: (310) 393-4818
website: www.rand.org

The Rand Corporation is a nonprofit research organization that performs policy analysis on critical social and economic issues such as education, poverty, crime, and the environment, as well as a range of national security issues.

Reason Foundation

3415 S. Sepulveda Blvd., Suite 400, Los Angeles, CA   90034
(310) 391-2245 • fax: (310) 391-4395
website: www.reason.org

The libertarian Reason Foundation works to provide a better understanding of the intellectual basis of a free society and to develop new ideas in public policy making. It researches contemporary social, economic, urban, and political problems. It publishes the newsletter *Privatization Watch* monthly and *Reason* magazine eleven times a year.

Republican National Committee

310 First St. SE, Washington, DC   20003
(202) 863-8500 • fax: (202) 863-8820
e-mail: info@gop.com
website: www.gop.com

The Republican National Committee is the principal organization governing the Republican Party, one of the two main political parties in the United States. The organization's website includes the party platform, news articles, and other articles and publications.

Socialist Party USA

339 Lafayette St. #303, New York, NY   10012
e-mail: natsec@socialistparty-usa.org
website: www.socialistparty-usa.org

The Socialist Party USA strives to establish a radical democracy that places people's lives under their own control. The party likewise strives for a democracy where working people own and control the means of production and distribution, where full employment is realized for everyone who wants to work, where workers have the right to form unions freely and to strike and engage in other forms of job actions, and where the production of society is used for the benefit of all humanity not for the private profit of a few.

Bibliography

Books

Glenn Beck · *America's March to Socialism: Why We're One Step Closer to Giant Missile Parades*. New York: Simon & Schuster, 2009.

William H. Boyer · *Myth America: Democracy vs. Capitalism*. New York: Apex, 2003.

G.A. Cohen · *Why Not Socialism?* Princeton, NJ: Princeton University Press, 2009.

Newt Gingrich · *To Save America: Stopping Obama's Secular-Socialist Machine*. Washington, DC: Regnery, 2010.

Aaron Klein and Brenda J. Elliott · *The Manchurian President: Barack Obama's Ties to Communists, Socialists, and Other Anti-American Extremists*. Washington, DC: WND, 2010.

Stanley Kurtz · *Radical-in-Chief: Barack Obama and the Untold Story of American Socialism*. New York: Simon & Schuster, 2010.

Michael Lebowitz · *The Socialist Alternative: Real Human Development*. New York: Monthly Review Press, 2010.

Alan Maass · *The Case for Socialism*. Chicago: Haymarket, 2010.

John MacKaye   *Americanized Socialism: A Yankee View of Capitalism.* New York: Boni and Liveright, 1918.

Joshua Muravchik   *Heaven on Earth: The Rise and Fall of Socialism.* San Francisco: Encounter, 2002.

Michael Newman   *Socialism: A Very Short Introduction.* New York: Oxford University Press, 2005.

John Ross   *Murdered by Capitalism: A Memoir of 150 Years of Life and Death on the American Left.* New York: Nation, 2004.

Joseph A. Schumpeter   *Capitalism, Socialism, and Democracy.* New York: HarperCollins, 2008.

Walter Williams   *Liberty Versus the Tyranny of Socialism: Controversial Essays.* Stanford, CA: Hoover Institution Press, 2008.

Lijia Zhang   *"Socialism Is Great!": A Worker's Memoir of New China.* New York: Anchor Books, 2009.

Periodicals and Internet Sources

Aram Bakshian Jr.   "Bends in the Curve," *American Spectator*, May 2010.

Beef   "No Confusion on Socialism vs. Capitalism," July 1, 2010. www.beefmagazine.com.

Simon Black — "Sports, Spectacle, and Socialism? A Conversation with Urban Scholar and Activist Roger Keil," *Canadian Dimension*, May–June 2010.

Paul Bond — "Socialism, Obama, and O'Donnell," *Hollywood Reporter*, September 17, 2010.

Christopher Caldwell — "Victory Lap; Final Reflections on Communism's Failure," *Weekly Standard*, March 1, 2010.

Howard Fineman — "'Socialism' Chicago Style," *Newsweek*, April 5, 2010.

David A. Graham — "Socialism Thrives in North Dakota," *Newsweek*, May 3, 2010.

Joshua Green — "Man Inside," *Atlantic*, April 2010.

Godfrey Hodgson — "Fighting the Spectre of the Far Right," *New Statesman*, June 10, 2002.

William F. Jasper — "The Grasp of Socialist International," *New American*, March 1, 2010.

Herbert London — "Sweden Is a Perfect Example of Socialism Run Amok," *Newsmax*, June 18, 2010.

Amory B. Lovins — "Nuclear Socialism: Energy Subsidies—of Any Kind—Are Bad Business," *Weekly Standard*, October 25, 2010.

Stephen Marche — "What's So Bad About Socialism Anyway?," *Esquire*, February 2009.

Kathy McGourty   "Is Social Justice the Same as Socialism?," *U.S. Catholic*, September 2010.

John F. McManus   "Mount Vernon Statement Shoptalk," *New American*, March 29, 2010.

Lauren Murrow   "Sidewalk Socialism," *New York*, July 12, 2010.

Matthew Poletti   "Grabbing Power in Venezuela," *Military Periscope Special Reports*, March 29, 2010.

Geoffrey Wheatcroft   "Nanny Doesn't Know Best," *New Statesman*, March 29, 2010.

Peter Wilby   "Star Pupils and Self-Service Socialists," *New Statesman*, August 23, 2010.

Index